Thank God I
Went Through Hell

Stories of Inspiration for Every Situation

Published by ThankGodi.com

http://www.thankgodi.com

ISBN: 978-0-9815453-4-9 (softcover)
978-0-9815453-6-3 (ebook)

Cover Design: Gio Sebastian

Special Thanks to Lorraine Garnett
and Jenetta Barry

Table of Contents

Introduction

*C*utting off people's clitorises and sewing up their vaginas?

The earth is filled with some sick shit, some really cruel insanity.

There's certainly no shortage of pain and suffering.

The truth is we HAD to create the ***Thank God I Went Through Hell*** series.

Why? A couple of decades ago, we decided to explore a simple yet profound principle.

That Principle?

We all experience unique challenges in our life. What appears to be true is that our individual life challenges repeat over and over, until we discover how these challenges are actually of perfect service to us. In essence, we overcome our challenges by becoming grateful for our challenges.

We know this may sound crazy at first, but we promise that as you explore these real-life stories, you'll start noticing some amazing changes in your own life. Even challenges as devastating as brutal rape, loss of a loved one, or even facing your own imminent death—though tremendously difficult—

1

hold within them hidden gifts that, when faced, liberate our spirit and transform our entire lives.

Thank God I Went Through Hell connects straight to your heart to help you re-discover the greatest healer of all… the love that is already present inside you. These amazing stories share actual solutions that show how it is possible to heal your heart and live an inspired life.

The human spirit is truly remarkable when faced with devastating events. Just when we think we're at our breaking point, we discover we're stronger than we knew. We find the courage to face our own demons.

These stories reveal the indomitable human spirit. An indomitable spirit that already exists inside you. You will read amazing insights from authors ranging from N.Y. Times best-seller Dr. Bernie Siegel to everyday people around the world who share precisely how they overcame situations that once seemed insurmountable.

Thank God I Went Through Hell is a collection of true, personal stories by people who have turned their real-life nightmares into extraordinary opportunities.

We believe that everyone deserves the information that will help them overcome their life challenges. That's why we have decided to give away the entire ***Thank God I Went Through Hell*** series for free. Please visit our website at www.thankgodi.com and feel free to share it with any of your friends.

Thank you for serving with us.

Thank God My Infertility Almost Killed Me

BY BELLA TISHKOVA

"Get her into the operating room NOW!"

*E*veryone madly running around … a life-threatening situation … immediate action required … NOW!

Could this have been me they were frantic about?

I came to in the recovery room. It felt like pure hell. I couldn't sit, drink, or even talk. Every cell in my body hurt ...

But I'm getting ahead of myself ...

While my life had never been a fairytale, after moving to the US from Russia, I felt I had made so much progress. I felt blessed. I was 27 years old, happily married, had a good career, and owned and lived in a new, beautifully remodeled house in which we had planned and created a pink baby room.

Here I was living the life I had always dreamed of. But the most important part of it was very much missing– we had no baby.

Month after month, our house was filled with ovulation kits, thermometers, calendars and charts, as we worked through the process of IVP, but it just wasn't happening.

Desperation overtook me at the end of each monthly cycle when, yet again, I was not pregnant. I felt a deep sense of loss for something I never had. It increased as all my friends gave birth, began raising their children, and then talked of birthday parties and posted their kids' achievements on Facebook. I was beyond desperate to become a part of that "mommy" inner circle.

Then one day something happened …

It began as a usual Saturday morning, but the moment I tried to get out of bed I felt a searing pain in my abdomen. It took a huge amount of effort to pull myself out of bed. As I walked downstairs to get some pain meds, my whole body became weightless, and with a spinning head, I passed out.

I came to, finding myself lying on top of the stairs. I could feel that something was very wrong with me. Overwhelmed with panic, I had a sense I might be dying.

But when I was rushed into the medical rooms and my obstetrician said with a smile, *"Let's do your first sonogram,"* my heart skipped a beat.

"OMG," my mind raced, *"It's really happening … they're doing a scan because I'm pregnant!"*

I lay there feeling mounting excitement– many thoughts flashing through my mind: *"These symptoms are because I am pregnant! I'm going to be a mommy! A little human being is growing inside me. I'll be able to feel that weird feeling of the baby moving inside!"*

My joy was cut short.

Within seconds, the sonogram revealed a big problem. My baby was growing in my fallopian tube, and this was causing bleeding. My abdomen was filled with blood, and my fallopian tube was about to rupture.

Bright lights, people in white running around...and my mind at a standstill.

I woke up with indescribable pain. I realized that what hurt more than the physical pain was my realization that I had just had a C-section, which had not produced a baby.

I'd been so close to finally experiencing a pregnancy, to becoming a mommy, to experiencing the joy of bringing a new little person into the world– I couldn't fathom why this should have happened to me.

I tried to reason that I could not have lost something I didn't have to begin with.

Yet no reasoning could remove my very deep emotional pain—it was so intense. I ached with overwhelm, wondering whether this lost baby would have been a boy or a girl. Wondering what it would have felt like to hold this little person in my arms. Now I would never know.

I felt empty inside and out. Even the house, where nothing had changed, felt dark. My whole body ached from both physical and emotional pain. I felt the most comfortable in my dark, quiet bedroom with my phone off. Trips to the bathroom were agonizingly painful. I refused to take my pain meds and my fresh stitches burned with every step. In order to get to the bathroom, I had to pass by my baby's pretty pink room.

I just couldn't come out of that dark place.

In those first few days and weeks, I remember my husband softly stroking my hair while gently coaxing me to get out of bed. Each morning he would cook me breakfast before going to work and on some days, he literally spoon-fed me.

The weeks turned into months. The ache eased a little with time. A year passed. And another ... and another ... still no baby. Until one day, those two familiar lines appeared on my pregnancy test, and with a surge of nervous excitement I realized that I was pregnant again. Simultaneously, in that moment of joy, I felt a stab of worry. The dread diluted my excitement, as I worried that this pregnancy would all go wrong again. My anxiety grew. In an attempt to calm myself down, I reasoned that lightning doesn't strike twice, so the chances of this pregnancy going wrong as well were slight.

Two agonizingly slow weeks of blood tests and sonograms followed. Then one morning, I once again felt that familiar abdominal pain. Again, I found myself shaking from head to toe in the very same nightmare situation.

Once again, panic in the operating room and feeling cold on the surgical table. I silently shouted from somewhere deep inside me, *"This can't be happening again!"* I lay there hoping I was in a bad dream. If only I could just wake up ...

After surgery, I went through that same sense of deep loss—of mourning for another lost little being—and realizing with dread that I had more days, months, years of coping and overcoming. With time, I painfully resigned myself to accept that I was more than likely never going to be able to experience pregnancy or parenthood.

Even so, we decided to continue to try to fall pregnant.

Again, weeks, months, years passed ... in fact, four whole years ... and then one day ... I found I was pregnant once again. This time, with just as much anguish as before, I went through all the medical tests and my little person began to grow.

At long last, I experienced the amazing joy of the first butterfly flutters of movement. I watched my belly expand. I experienced every part of my pregnancy. My heart soared when I finally gave birth and my beautiful daughter, Alice Aleksandra, was placed in my arms.

To this day, my mind is not able to comprehend that I was successfully pregnant. As I put her to bed each night and kiss her tiny nose, my whole heart fills with love, gratitude, and appreciation for human life.

On overall reflection, I am able to now understand how my imperfect adversity has perfectly brought me to a level of love as a parent that I would never have reached had I just fallen pregnant and birthed my child. I used to wonder why humans have to go through so much hardship, but now I see a bigger picture. I understand that the destruction in my life has brought me to a new way of living—through my despair, I've been given an innate ability to overcome life's challenges and keep moving ahead.

This has since helped me to become even more in tune with my precious relationships. It has opened deep, empathetic conversations with my sister and mother. When I was in the deepest parts of my pain, it felt as if my mother and I were one.

I also learned a depth of patience, of stoic determination and a deeper faith and trust that adversity can be worked through. These skills now assist me every day in my work with children with autism and their families. Another outcome is that I have been able to help many would-be moms who are struggling to become pregnant.

But the greatest gift from within this adversity has been my husband's and my relationship. Our adversity enabled him to show me levels of patience, kindness, love, and understanding. This helped me to experience a side of him I had never known.

Shortly after my first unsuccessful pregnancy, my husband was diagnosed with cancer. For nine years we have been fighting this devastating disease. In the past two years it spread, and our doctors don't have any positive prognosis for us. Now I have a chance to be by his side and treat him with the same kindness and patience that I was treated with by him.

I am deeply grateful for the *"hell"* we went through with my infertility and pregnancy losses. Those experiences, have brought us to a depth of understanding that would have been missing in dealing with our current life challenge. Because of what we had previously been through, we are able to just sit next to each other on the couch watching some silly TV show and just feel each other's pain. And despite the pain, it feels so peaceful, warm and easy to breathe. When I feel his shoulder next to me, I feel safe and complete. And the level of connection and understanding and trust is so remarkably deep, that no words are needed anyway. I feel incredibly blessed for the opportunity to be his partner, his best friend, and his wife.

♡♡♡

*At the age of 20, **Bella Tishkova** immigrated to the US from Russia. With no money and no place to live she single-handedly built her new life and at the same time, completed 2 Masters degrees in Education and entered a Ph.D. program at Columbia University.*

She is a Special Educator and school Administrator and has worked as an Intervention Evaluator and Therapist with children and families affected with and by Autism. She has also trained and worked closely with therapists as a Program Supervisor.

Bella is currently training with ThankGodi to become a Certified Equilibration Consultant. Bella lives with her husband Paul and daughter Alice, in Brooklyn, New York.

Thank God I'm Blind

BY BEN UNDERWOOD

*I*n 1994 at age two I lost my eyes to a childhood disease called Retinoblastoma—which is cancer in both eyes. At age three I taught myself Echolocation—where I use sound to see. I ride bikes, skate, and play video games. You name it, I do it. Or at least give it a try.

It isn't so bad being blind—you just learn to see differently.

I'll tell you the truth: being blind is more of an "advantage." I don't see what you see, but I've learned how to see with eyes closed. I have to see others for who they are by their hearts—whether no eyes, no legs, autistic, mentally challenged, or whatever the difference is, we are truly all the same. God loves each one of us unconditionally and wants us to learn to see one another through the eyes of God.

Believing and drawing closer to Jesus is how I became softhearted—to the point where I care. Seeing what you see every day, you have become used to the "torture" that others go through. I do not "see" these things. I do know what is going on, but not seeing these tortures helps me stay a more loving and kind-hearted person. I thank God I'm blind because I see others for who they are by their hearts, and you see one another with your eyes, which sometimes are blinded. I remind those going through trying times in their lives that there are still people concerned about them.

God loves each one of us unconditionally and wants us to learn to see one another through the eyes of God. Sometimes looking through a blind person's eyes can truly teach us to see each other as we see ourselves.

I was again diagnosed with this cancer—retinoblastoma (this time without eyes)—at age 16. This cancer started in the sinus cavity and entered my brain, but was still the same ordeal that I endured when I was two years old. Going through cancer this time, I lost my hair from the chemo treatments, and I have a scar from ear-to-ear from the surgery.

Through all that I've endured, I thank God I'm blind. I can't actually see what these changes in my appearance look like—so it doesn't matter. I hear others crying because of their hair loss, or scarring, worried what other people will think about their looks. I don't worry about my appearance—I can't see. Thank God I am blind.

When I was 13, I went to a school for the blind for my seventh grade school year. My mother thought it would be a good idea for me to experience being around other blind children. This school wasn't in Sacramento where I lived, so I had to leave home every Sunday in the early evening, and come home Friday night—only to be home on the weekends.

They taught me a lot of technology, math, and other learning activities. We also went to the local junior high for a couple of classes every day. As a teenager I learned

how blind individuals are treated—or maybe the word is
taught.

My experience there wasn't very enjoyable. I found out
that blind people are expected to "be" a certain way.
Blind students at this school traveled in groups: the guide
was in front with the cane going left to right, with
everyone else kind of holding onto one another, trusting
the front cane traveler to guide the rest. Well, I hadn't
traveled like this before. I traveled independent of a cane,
or used a sighted guide like my brother or a friend. Once I
brought a big rubber ball to the school, and was told that I
couldn't bring balls because someone might get hurt. I
thought all kids played with balls.

I called my mom and told her that I couldn't go to this
school because I wasn't like them. I don't consider myself
blind—I just can't see. You see, my family didn't tell me
there was anything different about being blind or sighted.
They treat me just like a sighted person. I guess I consider
myself sighted in a way because I believe anything that
you can do—I can do better. I kept encouraging the staff
that blind kids can play ball, video games, and other
activities that sighted kids do. I continued to insist that we
be treated like everyone else. After consistently pursuing
equality of treatment for the blind, the staff finally
softened up and began to allow the blind students to do
more outside activities. One thing I enjoyed about the
school for the blind was that the students didn't judge one
another on their appearance—because no one could see.
That was actually a very good attribute. What a great
experience. Thank God I'm blind.

Once my mother asked me what it was like being blind.
She thought that if she turned out the light in the
bathroom and closed her eyes—that would be similar to

being blind. I told her that it wasn't the same. For me being blind is actually "nothingness." I don't think that a sighted person can comprehend what nothingness looks like. Although my sight is nothingness, my mother has described the world to me and showed me what things look like. Because of my family, I actually have a "visual" of the world.

While they showed me the world, they showed me independence. When my brother Derius was eight years old, he taught me how to find my tags and the seams of my clothing so that I could dress myself properly. My sister Tiffany has been there for me. My brother Isaiah is three years younger than I am and he showed me everything he saw. Joe is my oldest brother—and he thought he was my "daddy." He tried to tell me what to do—so we fought all the time. I love my family because they see me the same as they are—not as a blind brother but as their brother. My family has been there for me. They treat me in such a way that I can echo—and no one complains about the sound. I think they don't complain because with my echo I can ride my own bike—and none of them has to ride me. I think they made sure that I was self-sufficient because it gave them the freedom of not having to take care of me. I am so glad that they did what they did.

Sometimes I feel sorry for blind kids who don't get the opportunity to enjoy their childhood as a child should. I thank God I'm blind. I've heard from people all around the world about my echolocation. Most people are truly encouraged about me being independent and using echolocation. However, some blind people feel that I am "mocking the blind." I just want to tell the world that I don't have anything against using a cane—it just isn't for me. I'm 16 years old and the cane sort of gets in my way when I'm "traveling." I do understand that there are "blind" world travelers, professors, and very successful blind individuals, and I pray that as our world continues to turn, individuals are not categorized by their disability. I feel that we should look at each individual's "difference" and not see a "disability." As God's creation, we need to learn to love and encourage one another—not discourage a person who doesn't look like you, walk, talk, nor see like you. No one deserves to be categorized and put in a disability box. Because I'm blind I don't see the appearance of a person—I see beyond that. I see individuals for who and what they are. I truly THANK GOD I'M BLIND.

♡♡♡

*"Faith in God." That is what **Ben Underwood** was about. On January 19, 2009, after the return of his cancer, Ben's life on this earth came to a quiet end. Like a tiny mustard seed, Ben's initial faith in life grew to incredible proportions. Like the parable of the mustard tree, he stretched out as far as possible, bearing amazing fruit. He planted his seeds of faith and, for all who came in contact with him, watered them with inspiration. Ben was known worldwide through his creation of echolocation, a clicking sound created by his tongue that allowed him to visualize objects and surroundings. Speaking engagements in Germany, Japan, and Amsterdam—and media exposure across the globe—made Ben Underwood inspiration for millions. Appearances of this extraordinary young man on CBS, ABC, CNN, the Ellen Degeneres Show, the Montell Williams Show, and the Oprah Winfrey Show amazed America. To his large, loving family, he was simply Ben. Never afraid of*

anything, Ben did anything he ever set his mind on. He rode bikes, played ball, practiced karate, danced, and loved making music—especially on the ocarina. Ben had written since the age of eight and created a children's book and a story series that may be available soon. Thank God he shared his story with us.

Learn more about Ben at www.benunderwood.com.

Thank God I Was a Racist

BY BRUCE MUZIK

I pulled up to my new home and felt terror in the pit of my stomach. But, I knew I had to go through with this. I saw the same fear in Dad's eyes. *"Are you sure you really want to do this?"* he asked. I nodded and got out of the car. Next door, two people sat on empty beer crates, drinking beer, on the otherwise deserted street. I wanted to move into my new home quietly, with time to adjust to my new surroundings.

But it was too late. The beer drinkers came over to find out why Dad and I were unloading boxes from my truck. Another local arrived to watch, and within minutes, twenty-five starring people surrounded us, faces as black as night. One of them, a woman, came forward, *"Umlungu* ('white man,' in the Xhosa tongue), *what you doing?"*

"I'm moving in," I told her warily as I pointed toward the dilapidated "shantytown" house that was my home for the next thirty days. I sensed her confusion as she turned to the others and translated what I'd said into Xhosa, their native language. As if in slow motion, the looks upon their faces turned from curiosity to disbelief. The crowd murmured in unison as they grappled with the concept of a white man moving into their black community in the

16

township of Guguletu, the African equivalent of a ghetto or shantytown. Unsure of my real motives, the woman introduced herself to me as Maureen, my new neighbor. *"What do you mean you are moving in?"* Maureen asked.

I decided to tell the truth, as difficult as it was for me to admit.

"I recently discovered that I'm a racist," I told her boldly, not wanting her to know how terrified I was, *"and I'm moving into Guguletu to learn about your culture and conquer my fear of black people."* A look of shock crossed their faces.

Two weeks earlier, I'd stood in front of a room filled with a hundred and ten people in a personal development course, clutching a microphone. David, the wonderfully powerful man leading the course, said,

"How many black friends do you have, Bruce?"

"Uh, three," I lied, not wanting to admit that, in fact, I didn't have any close black friends. It wasn't that I didn't like black people, it's just that I never made the time to get to know any of them on more than a superficial level.

"You mean to say that you live in a country where eighty percent of the population is black—that's 40 million people—and you are friendly with only three of them?" David asked incredulously, pacing his words for maximum effect. A hush fell over the room as David patiently waited for his words to sink in and for me to answer.

Put that way, it did sound ridiculous. I laughed nervously as the reality of David's question revealed my hypocrisy.

For years, I'd despised the apartheid regime in South Africa, and when the country finally had its first democratic elections in 1994, I rejoiced and proudly claimed my title as a New South African. Now, nine years on, I still did not have any.

"I think I'm just scared of getting to know them," I admitted.

The apartheid government of the "old" South Africa conditioned us to believe that black people were third-class citizens, while white people were first-class citizens. In my growing up years, the media taught us to fear black people. On a subconscious level, this fear became normal for me, even though consciously I knew it to be wrong. I grew up in an area surrounded by imposing brick walls with electric fences to keep black people out. Black people perpetrated most of the crimes reported by the newspapers. I learned to lock the doors of my car to make sure that nobody hijacked it, and although never spoken aloud, nobody ever expected a white person to hijack a car. My local beach had an intimidating fence down the middle, separating the huge, sandy "white" beach from the much smaller, rocky "black" beach. We had buses for whites and buses for blacks. At one point in time, black people could not walk on the streets after 7 p.m.

"So, Bruce, would you like to get to know some of your fellow black South Africans?" David asked. I nodded introspectively, and David continued, *"How are you going to do that?"*

"Well, I guess I can go and talk to them. I can chat with the car guards outside my office, and I'll even sponsor some of them to do this course if they want to," I replied, excited at the prospect of completing this uncomfortable

conversation and getting back to the anonymity of my seat in the audience.

"Well, that'll make you feel good for a few days, but it certainly won't change your life or your attitude to black people, will it?" I knew David was right, but I felt awkward and put on the spot.

Aargh! Where was he going with this? *"What's the best way to get to know someone?"* David asked.

"Live with them?" I answered tentatively.

"That might do it. Why not go and live with some black people and get over your fear of them?" This suggestion was too much for me. Was he insane? How could a white guy go and live in an African township? How ridiculous.

I thanked David for his advice and returned to the safety of my seat. The rest of that day was hell for me. He'd challenged me to go and live with black people, and I'd chickened out. I was a coward, and I knew it. I hated the feeling. That night I slept restlessly and awoke early to return to the course. At breakfast, my landlady, whose luxury three-story mansion I was house-sitting at the time, informed me that she'd be traveling for six months and planned to lock up the house. She gave me six weeks' notice to move out and find a new place to live. This was just too synchronous to be coincidence. Yesterday I was challenged to live with black people, and today I am asked to move? Slowly it dawned on me that perhaps the Powers That Be wanted me to take David up on his challenge and move to an African township.

Now, two weeks later, here I was moving into an area called the "Kak Yard" (crap yard), which earned its name because its crime-ridden streets were once inhabited by the "scum" of society in the township of Guguletu, just outside Cape Town. As far as I know, I was the only white man for miles among tens of thousands of black people.

Maureen looked visibly shocked to hear my admission of being a racist. She translated to the now-baffled and suspicious locals who, after a few seconds of silence, proceeded to laugh as if this was the funniest joke they had ever heard. I later found out that some of them suspected I was a part of a secret police operation sent to infiltrate. *"Can we help you carry your boxes into the house?"* Maureen offered, catching me off guard.

Oh, crap! Now I am truly screwed. I thought to myself. If I don't let them carry my boxes, they'll be offended and reject me from their community. That's just what I don't want. However, if I do let them carry my boxes, they are going to steal them. I caught myself mid-thought as I recognized my racist conditioning taking control of my mind again. This was just what I had come here to conquer. *"Sure"* I replied *"why not?"*

Several white-toothed, grinning new neighbors walked toward me and proceeded to haul my boxes off my truck into my new home. As I walked into my "new" dilapidated home, we were greeted by hundreds of cockroaches and a damp, moldy smell. Although definitely several steps down from the luxury mansion I had been living in, I wasn't bothered. I wanted an authentic African experience, and this was definitely it!

Maureen and my new neighbors stacked my boxes neatly in a corner of the living room, and the celebrations began. The welcome party that ensued was unlike any I've experienced. For the next two hours, they hugged, kissed, questioned, fed, and generally treated me like the prodigal son returning home. My neighbors' unconditional generosity and love overwhelmed me. I'll never forget the image of two enormous African women sprinting down the road, their voluptuous bodies heaving in slow motion as they closed in on me shouting *"Umlungu, Umlungu!"* (*"Whitey! Whitey!"*). News had already spread that a white man was moving in, and they were coming to say hello. Before I could escape, they ran into me, almost knocking me over with their huge, welcoming hugs. This was going better than I'd expected.

For a moment, I knew how celebrities must feel. I hoped to make friends, but never in a million years could I have predicted this kind of welcome. During those first two hours in Guguletu, I peeled away layer upon layer of racial conditioning, and I learned more about South African culture than most white South Africans learn in a lifetime. I went to bed that night listening to the foreign sounds of Guguletu street life. I couldn't decide if I was scared or if I was excited, but decided I was probably both.

The next morning, I woke up with a familiar feeling growing in the pit of my stomach. The reality of my circumstance sunk in, and I wanted to hide away in bed all day. I forced myself to go outside and eat my breakfast sitting on the front steps of my house. As I watched the locals scurry off to work, a small child, dressed in a school uniform, walked past me. He stopped dead in his tracks when he saw me, obviously shocked to see a white face eating breakfast in his township. *"Do you live here?"* he asked.

"Yes," I replied.

He looked away, paused for a second, then turned to me and said with wisdom beyond his years *"Welcome home."* He turned away and continued his walk to school. Tears rolled down my cheeks as thirty years of racial prejudice evaporated in that instant. I was home. A few days later, while I supported a local football team in Guguletu, a spectator came up to me and announced, *"You need a Xhosa name. From now on, you will be called Xolani."*

"What does that mean?" I asked curiously.

"Xolani means bringer of peace," he replied, smiling. I liked it.

From that day on, I stopped introducing myself as Bruce. I was now Xolani. I felt proud to have an African name, and I loved seeing my neighbors' delight when I introduced myself as Xolani.

One month came and went. Living in Guguletu was such a meaningful experience for me that I stayed for six incredible months. I returned with new eyes to my old life. During those six months, my community and I both learned that despite the difference in our culture and skin color, we are all the same. I learned about community when my neighbors risked their lives to save mine, fighting off a gang of thieves who attacked me one night in an attempt to steal my phone.

I learned about love when, while I was drinking at a shabeen (an illegal bar in someone's home) on the other side of Guguletu, Maureen arrived, having walked 2 kilometers at night through the most dangerous part of Guguletu, just to check up on me and make sure I was OK.

I learned humility and determination as I turned hundreds of beggars away empty-handed, instead offering to teach them to earn their own money. In six months, only one accepted my offer. I learned about trust when I accepted Maureen's offer to look after my house and possessions as I traveled abroad to visit my family. I came back to find my house in better shape than when I had left!

Those six months changed me, changed my community, silenced my prejudices, and brought me humbly to my knees. I now have so many black friends I couldn't begin to count them. In retrospect, I thank God I was a racist, and I thank God I had the opportunity to learn these lessons—to learn what home, community, and Africa truly are.

♡♡♡

Bruce Muzik—"The Couples Whisperer"—has built a reputation as the guy relationship counselors refer their toughest clients to, to help fix their troubled marriages. Unlike most traditional relationship advisers who advocate learning communication skills, Bruce believes most people already know how to communicate, but have never learned how to stay emotionally connected to each other.

Visit Bruce at www.LoveAtFirstFight.com and grab his free instructional videos on how to stop fighting and start being happy together. His TEDx talk has been watched more than 1 million times and can be watched at: http://www.BruceMuzik.com/tedx/

Thank God I Had Cancer

BY CASSANDRA GATZOW

*I*t was about 3:00 p.m. on September 15, 2006, when I got the call. I was in the midst of my working day, about to walk into one of my accounts. I worked as a salon consultant for a beauty distribution company at the time.

About a month and a half earlier, I'd had a wink from God take place in my life. While doing a late spring cleaning, I somehow decided my birth control pills had expired. The date read May 2007, and it was only May 2006, but for some reason, I thought we were in 2007. So I grabbed the pills and tossed them in the trash. About a month later, as my pack was ending, I looked at the date again and realized what I had done. So I scheduled an appointment with my gynecologist for July and went on with my business.

My GYN found some abnormal cells, which resulted in more tests, more appointments. This, in turn, led up to the phone call. I sat in the accountant's parking lot when the call came in: My gynecologist had my biopsy results. Being twenty-two at the time and never having been sick a day in my life, I could not even fathom what she said next. First asking if I was in a place to talk, she told me that I had full-blown cancer developing in me. She said

24

there was nothing more she could do, and I needed to contact a specialist. After giving me his name and number, she wished me good luck. I sat in my car and just about lost feeling in every inch of my body.

That night and the days to follow were a blur. I had to tell my family and my friends. I had to notify my work and make an appointment to see this doctor. Three days later, I sat in his office and awaited my future. He told me that I had cervical cancer, rather large, and that it had invaded both sides. I had only one option—undergo a hysterectomy in nine days. Then, based on the results of that, I might proceed with treatment.

Many members of my family have been lost to cancer, so the very word created a large, open wound within my family and me. One of my grandmothers is a survivor of seven years, but the other four members of my family were not so lucky. I remember being twelve and standing by my other grandmother's hospital bed just moments before she passed. She was in such horrible pain, and we could do nothing.

I could feel the wound start to bleed in all of us as the process began.

Those nine days seemed to go by slowly, and my heart broke every time I had a moment with a loved one. The hardest conversation I had was with my sixteen-year-old brother. My heart ripped when tears filled his eyes and he asked if I was going to die. I grabbed him and told him I was going to be just fine—we had to take it one day at a time. That is what I continued to tell myself as the days passed. It took me a week to tell the man I loved. The strong woman I once knew was scattered and scared to death.

The day of my surgery was an interesting one. I had to be at the hospital at 9:00 a.m. for surgery at 11:00 a.m. My boyfriend, David, and I arrived at the hospital, with him as sick as can be. He was shaking and throwing up. I had no idea what was wrong with him. The whole thing going on with him did take my mind off me. It allowed me to go into caring mode. He was quickly sent to emergency and away from me. A few moments later, they wheeled me into the elevator on a gurney, toward the preparation room. While we were in the elevator, I told my mother not to worry ... I would be just fine. She was overwhelmed with tears. I can't explain the peace that came over me that morning, or the peace that has stayed with me since. It was as if angels' wings were holding me.

I awoke from surgery to find a tube in my nose and several beeping machines surrounding me. I was freezing cold and couldn't stop shaking. Shortly after, they wheeled me up to my room, where my sweet mother and family waited for me.

David was nowhere to be found. I got a phone call from him about an hour later, saying, *"Honey, I was right beside you in the recovery room. I had my appendix removed!"* There he was, a floor under me, with the same tummy scars as me.

I remained in the hospital for a week due to the intensity of the surgery. The healing process would be a long one, with more to it than I thought. Having David in the hospital with me those first three days was wonderful. I was so heartbroken about what I had been through and what was going to happen next. His smile gave me hope. It's interesting how the Universe works. The people who have surrounded me, since the beginning are truly earth angels. Three weeks passed, and I was back in my doctor's office awaiting the news. I was ready to move past this event and get on with my emotional and physical healing. I had to deal with not being able to bear children and the feeling that I had been robbed of my innocence. I was only twenty-two, and what work I had ahead of me!

Well, it wasn't quite over yet. My doctor informed me that the cancer had spread to the outside tissues, and the only way to ensure that it was gone was with chemotherapy and radiation. At the moment those two words were spoken, I once again lost all feeling in my being. My doctor told me that I was very special and was going to make it through.

"Well, okay then," I said, *"but I must go back to work so I can feel normal in some way."*

He referred me to a chemotherapy specialist and a radiation center. My soul burned through my eyes, and I knew I was not ready to go. I lasted three days on the pills and decided I would rather be in pain.

I returned to work, and about a week later I went in to see the specialist about starting treatment. They performed various scans and tests, and I was ready to get started in a week. In the process of waiting, I continued working while experiencing the most incredible pain in my side. When I returned to start treatment and informed them of this pain, I had no clue what was in store for me. I was soon told, *"Your tumor has returned."* In the six weeks since surgery, my tumor had returned and was hitting some nerves on my side. So what now?

I started treatment and was put on some heavy-duty pain pills that I could not tolerate.

Once again I was not able to work and could barely even sleep. I looked in the mirror and had no idea who stood there. My soul burned through my eyes, and I knew it was not ready to go. I lasted three days on the pills and decided I would rather be in pain. I had chemo once a week for six weeks, while the radiation was daily. After my first treatment, I was hospitalized and told that I had one bad kidney. My ability to continue with the chemo depended on how my kidneys reacted to the treatments.

Every treatment was closely monitored.

There were times that I would lie on my bathroom floor and pray to leave my body. I've never felt such emotional and physical pain before. I couldn't sleep, I couldn't eat, and I couldn't care for myself. There were times that I was so weak I could barely brush my hair or shower. At the time I was living alone, so my mother moved in to care for me. With her help, along with David, and my dear friend, Laurie, I made it through all of my treatments.

What I thought was the end of the treatments, I learned was only the middle. I had yet to undergo two internal implants and another five-week course of external radiation.

Back to the hospital daily, and two more times being put under for the implants. I cannot find the words to explain how out of control I felt. I had to hand over my body to a medical staff. I had to open up and allow others to care for me. Both are things I had never had to do before. The process of being treated for cancer is an emotional and physical challenge. There were pieces of it that led me to want to leave my body. It truly was as though my soul led me and my body was being dragged along throughout this process.

One day as I walked on the beach outside my home, there was this energy and strength that rose out of the center of my being. It was as if I had awakened from a deep sleep. I realized how blessed I was to have this experience so young. My soul was speaking to me in a way that I could not understand until I was ready to listen. Throughout my treatments, I changed my thoughts and actions. I would dress up to go into my implant surgery and bake for the staff that cared for me the next couple of days. I decided to celebrate my life and become grateful for this experience. I would spend many days and nights alone, looking at my life—looking at who I was and who I wanted to be. I looked at who surrounded me and how beautiful the moments were that we spent together. My heart began to open, and I started to ask what I needed to learn.

This event came into my life to change my direction. It came to teach me something, and all the elements of it were designed especially for me. It was then that my spirit started to sing. I started to nurture myself. During this process I lost twenty-five pounds ... they flew right off me. I had also lost all my strength and confidence. It was that day on the beach that I decided to consciously pick up the pieces of Cassandra and put them back together again. In doing this, I was given the opportunity to look at them like I had never seen them before. Every day, my eyes filled with tears of gratitude for every moment and every breath. I started to walk more and laugh more. I started to work out with a group of cancer survivors and patients. I found the *"Thank God I ..."* project and began to live from my heart and step back to see what a beautiful life I had.

I am writing my story because cancer has changed my life. It has allowed me to go after my dreams, to live from my heart, and to truly be free. I thank God for my cancer and for allowing me to reach a place in myself that I don't think would have been possible without this experience. I am now twenty-three and feel that I have stepped into my skin proudly. I have felt an inner peace that many don't find until later in life. I am truly grateful for all my earth angels and want to thank them for sharing with me this wonderful journey.

It is in the moments of complete chaos that the most beautiful clarity comes to us. It is in becoming grateful for everything and loving every piece of it that you start to hear the truth. It is in that piece of frozen time that you can look back and see who you are. In the midst of this illness, which I was convinced would remove me from my physical body, I have come to embrace my body and feel comfort in it like never before. Learning to be grateful for this illness as it was happening to me, through every stage, has truly transformed me.

This *"Thank God I ..."* project has inspired me because it helped me remember to be grateful throughout my illness. It reminded me that I am here to heal others and to share what I have learned. As I am coming to a close of this process called "Cancer," I see how it was exactly what I needed to become Cassandra. It has allowed me to love every inch of myself, and in doing that, I can love every inch of you. I can appreciate and know that we all have our journeys and processes, but all serve and come for a reason. I thank God for my Cancer and for the opportunity to step into my new skin, skin that I wear proudly and cannot wait to share with you!

Peace and many blessings to each and every one of you.

♡♡♡

Cassandra Ann Gatzow *blessed this earth in her physical form by sharing wisdom that was well beyond her twenty-three precious years. Our angel's beautiful old soul touched numerous lives through her generous spirit of love, grace, and gratitude. Cassandra inspired us all to cherish every day by not taking anything for granted, and her message of compassion, joy, courage, and kindness remains reflected in all that she influenced.*

After a year-long fight with cervical cancer, Cassandra transitioned to continue her work in her spiritual form for God, humanity, and nature that extends well beyond this realm of life. Through Cassandra's sincere consciousness of "One Love," we can all feel her presence, shine her light, and make every day special and meaningful.

Live for Today! (Spoken for Cassandra through David Baumann)

Thank God I Am Not An Ugly Duckling

PART 1: AS TOLD BY DR. BERNIE SIEGEL TO HIS GRANDCHILDREN

*T*he other day, as I sat on our back porch enjoying the sun, a bedraggled little duck startled me with a big splash as he crash-landed in the little pond I built in our backyard. As he settled down and tried to catch his breath, I noticed his feathers that pointed in all directions. I continued to watch as our rabbit, Smudge, hopped over to the pond and struck up a conversation.

"Hi, I'm Smudge. If you're looking for a place to rest, you landed in the right place. Can I get you something to eat? You look tired and hungry."

"I could use a bite to eat and a few moments to catch my breath," said the little duck.

When Smudge gave me the sign, I took over some birdseed and corn from our food bin, then went back and sat down so I wouldn't frighten his new friend.

"That helped. Thanks!" said the little duck.

32

"Happy to help," Smudge replied. *"The humans who live here, Bobbie and Bernie, rescued my sister Snowflake and me two years ago. They have big hearts and a house full of animals that they love. We all have stories to tell. What's yours?"*

"When I popped out of the egg before I was expected," the duck explained, *"my mom told me that she was disappointed in me from day one because I was so small—and had weird-looking feathers. She said she was tired of explaining things to people and hiding me. She kept telling me what a disappointment I was to her and my dad. This broke my heart, so I decided to run away. I'm an ugly duckling with no place to run to."*

Without hesitation, Smudge replied, *"Well you have a place now. You stay right here while I tell everyone about you. We'll get you moved into our bird sanctuary where you'll get to meet the other ducks and geese who live here—not to mention all the other creatures we have rescued who have learned we're all family."*

"Why are you being so nice when you don't even know me?" asked the duckling.

"Dear Doctor Bernie taught us that we're all wounded and have our share of troubles. He's a surgeon and says we're all one family with the same color inside," explained Smudge. *"So we try to serve one another. I know someone whose childhood was a lot like yours, except for one thing that made all the difference in the world to him.*

"Would you like to hear a story? It might help you understand and change how you see yourself," asked Smudge.

"Sure. I'm definitely not going anywhere," said the duckling as he settled down to listen.

"Once upon a time," Smudge began *"there was a young woman who was told not to become pregnant because she was very sick and had lost a lot of weight. Her doctor felt becoming pregnant might endanger her life. She and her husband followed the doctor's advice, but her mother wouldn't accept it. She told her daughter to lie down on the couch, and she started feeding her all through the day. Well, in time, the woman gained thirty pounds—and went ahead and became pregnant.*

"Things went reasonably well until the time when the baby was due."

Smudge paused his story to say to the duckling, *"You showed up too soon, while this duckling seemed like he had no interest in ever coming out.*

"Weeks went by," he continued, *"and finally his mom went into labor, but after several days, he still didn't show his little head. I think it was his big head that was the problem—but don't tell anyone I told you that.*

"His mom was going through a lot of pain. The doctor said he really needed to get her baby out. But she wasn't well enough to risk a cesarean section—so they reached way up inside and pulled the baby out!

"Then the fun began. His mom said when she saw him, she thought, 'They didn't give me a baby; they gave me a purple melon!' So she and the baby's dad wrapped him in 'kerchiefs and put him in a covered carriage—so no one

*would see him—and when they got home, they hid his
carriage behind the house, then covered all the mirrors."*

"Boy, I know how he must have felt," the duckling
chipped in.

*"But there was one big difference between his family and
yours,"* Smudge continued. *"He didn't consider running
away from home. Can you guess why?"*

"No."

"Think about it," said Smudge, *"He had what you didn't
have—a grandmother. And he was her grandchild. She
saw the beauty that his parents hadn't learned how to see.*

"It's not their fault," added Smudge, *"and I am not
blaming anyone. It's about life and what they have
experienced. Hey, the next generation becomes great-
grandchildren, so it is definitely about what we learn from
our experience.*

*"I'm sure you know by now that the ugly duckling with a
grandmother was Bernie.*

*"Bernie's mom said her mother took him and poured oil
over him many times a day. She massaged and pushed
things back where they belonged. Bernie said that as he
grew up, whenever he worried about how he looked, he'd
go to his grandma for a hug. Finally, when he was old
enough to go to school for the first time, he told his
grandma, 'I don't know how I look. There are no mirrors
in our house.'*

*"She answered, 'Come over here. Look into my eyes and
you will see how beautiful you are.' Bernie didn't need*

plastic surgery, nor did he do what the ugly duckling did—run away from home. You won't have to struggle to see by your reflection that you are beautiful because you'll see that in our eyes. Bernie's grandma taught us all a few things. Bobbie (Bernie's wife) did insist upon having a mirror by their front door. So Bernie's grandmother hung a sign across the top of it that said -

'Come and see how beautiful and meaningful life is.'

"*So whenever anyone is having a 'bad' day—and Grandma isn't around—we just go and stand in front of Grandma's mirror.*"

PART 2: THE UGLY DUCKLING

Many years ago my mother—due to her hyperthyroidism—was told not to become pregnant because she had lost a great deal of weight, and her physician felt the added stress of pregnancy would endanger her health and life. Her mother—my future grandmother—didn't agree, and so she had my mother lie on the couch while she gorged her with food. My mother gained weight—and became pregnant.

As the due date drew close, my mother experienced an early rupture of her membrane—which she did not communicate to the doctor due to a lack of understanding. When she finally went into labor, I didn't seem interested in being delivered. After several days of labor and, to quote my mom, *"Screaming and tearing up all the hospital bed sheets,"* her doctor told her he felt a cesarean section was too risky to attempt—and they needed to get me out. So I presume they reached in with forceps and pulled me out.

My mother said, *"They didn't hand me a baby. They handed me a purple melon."* Yes, my mother was handed an ugly duckling. What do you do when you give birth to an ugly duckling?

In the story above, we are told the duckling's mother rejects him and eventually discards him from the nest.

When I read the story to our grandchildren, I thought about how rare it is for an ugly duckling ever to look at his or her reflection and accept being a swan. Even swans look in the mirror and find their faults—and not their beauty. Studies show that ugly ducklings are far more likely to become addicts and self-destructive as they grow up. So what saved me?

My mother said that when they took me home from the hospital, my father wrapped me in 'kerchiefs. Once home, my mother covered my carriage and placed it behind the house so no one would see me and be upset. There are photographs in our family album showing my smiling mom standing next to a covered carriage, and no photographs of me, which proves this was true. So I told my mother I wanted to know why I turned out the way I did. My question was, *"How and why did I make it?"* *"What did I have that the ugly duckling didn't have?"*

The answer, of course, is a grandmother. I recall reading a story where a teenager living with her grandmother complained that there were no mirrors in the house so she couldn't tell how she looked before going off to high school. Her grandmother replied, *"Look in my eyes and you'll see how beautiful you are."* Well, my mother tells me my grandmother took me from her, and five or six times a day, *"Poured oil over you, and then pushed everything back where it belonged."* I had my answer. I was massaged by loving hands every few hours. I know what that touch does to newborns of all species. They gain weight and mature faster than their untouched siblings—or the "controls" when a study of the effect of massage on infants is done.

Several decades later—the first time a female massage therapist placed her oiled hands on my shaved head—I went into a trance which frightened everyone in the room because they were unable to communicate with me. When I came out of the trance and saw all the people in the room, I asked why they were all there. They said they thought I had a stroke or heart attack—because I was gone. I said, *"Yes, I was gone. I went back to my childhood because my body remembers what my grandmother did. I returned to my infancy because of the touch of a woman's hands."*

That event helped me to understand why I shaved my head early in life at a time when it was definitely not in style. So my advice to everyone—based upon my experience—is don't have children before the age of 60. Then you will be ready to love and not judge. I know this from my experience as a pediatric surgeon and as the father of five children, including twins, and as grandfather of eight grandchildren. I was very concerned regarding the physical integrity of our children—and even examined them after they were born. Yet I was only interested in loving our grandchildren when they were born. I was ready to deal with whatever came with them. That's when I understood why we call our children simply children, while the next generation becomes our grandchildren, and the generation after that becomes our great grandchildren. The reason for the various labels, I believe, relates to our development as loving human beings as the years pass. Hopefully, we will all act like loving grandparents someday. And on this day all the children will feel loved.

♡♡♡

Bernie Siegel, MD—*who prefers to be called Bernie—was born in Brooklyn, NY, and attended Colgate University and Cornell University Medical College, from which he* *graduated with honors. He holds membership in Phi Beta Kappa and Alpha Omega Alpha. His surgical training took place at Yale New Haven Hospital, West Haven Veteran's Hospital, and the Children's Hospital of Pittsburgh.*

For many, Bernie needs no introduction. He has touched many lives all over our planet. In 1978, he began talking about patient empowerment and the choice to live fully and die in peace. As a physician, who has cared for and counseled innumerable people whose mortality has been threatened by an illness, Bernie embraces a philosophy of living and dying that stands at the forefront of the medical ethics and spiritual issues our society grapples with today. He continues to assist in the breaking of new ground in the field of healing and personally struggling to live the message of kindness and love.

Bernie has been named one of the top 20 Spiritually Influential Living People on the Planet by the Watkins Review, which is published by Watkins Books, an esoteric bookshop in the heart of London, England. Established over 100 years ago, they are now one of the world's leading independent bookshops specializing in new, secondhand and antiquarian titles in the Mind, Body, Spirit field. He is listed in the top 100 Most Spiritually Influential Living People in The Watkins Top 100 Spiritual List.

Bernie has authored Love, Medicine & Miracles, Help Me To Heal, Children's book—365 Prescriptions For The Soul, 101 Exercises For The Soul, Love, Magic & Mud Pies, Buddy's Candle, Faith, Hope & Healing, poetry book—Words Swords, A Book of Miracles, The Art of Healing, and Love, Animals & Miracles.

www.BernieSiegelMD.com

Thank God I Have Gratitude

BY DR. JOHN DEMARTINI

*W*hat does it take to live "happily ever after?" Ask a hundred different people and you'll get a hundred different answers. While some claim happiness is simply being in a happy relationship, others believe winning a pile of money would allow them to live happily ever.

But, what if I told you that the hope for "happily ever after" is one of the greatest psychological and social delusions of our time? Winning a pile of money or having a great relationship won't keep you happy indefinitely, and half the time it might actually do the opposite. This might come as quite a shock!

If you set yourself up with the expectation that you are magically only going to live happily ever after, you may find yourself checking into a lifetime residence at the Heartbreak Hotel. Happiness-ever-after is a fantasy. It's a fairytale, and from this illusion are birthed some of the most prevalent social concerns including stress, suicide, heartache, hopelessness, anger, resentment, and depression.

41

Everlasting happiness goes against our truest nature. The purpose of life isn't to pursue only happiness, but to love and be grateful for life's winding road, which includes both happiness and sadness, positive and negative, and supportive and challenging experiences.

As you progress along your life voyage, you will experience life's natural cycles of highs and lows. However, the secret is to not fly too high on the up cycles or sink down too low on the down cycles. Instead, your purpose is to appreciate all of life's experiences (happy and sad) and grow from them by recognizing their inherent balance.

The secret is learning how to embrace the complete balance of life (no matter what form of high or low it takes). This allows you to find the blessings in every curse and teaches you how to be grateful with whatever confronts you in life.

So while you may not be able to live happily ever after, you can become deeply grateful in all areas of your life— no matter what happens. Let me tell you how to accomplish this "attitude of gratitude" in the seven areas of life:

Be Grateful For Your Spiritual State
With gratitude, you can open your heart to love. If you desire to love yourself, others, and your magnificent experience called life, then being grateful is one of the most important steps you can take.

Gratitude helps you live the life of your dreams. It doesn't matter if you are more conventional in your spiritual or religious beliefs or more orthodox—you can become grateful for the unseen energy flow of life that surrounds and fills you (the energy that some call the soul, others term the holy spirit, or what others refer to as the life force). Do not underestimate the power and depth that gratitude has.

Gratitude:
The key to experiencing love and fulfillment is connecting you to your own inner vital forces which you can bring into your everyday life.

Action steps:
Put aside a little time every day to connect with your inner spiritual force. It is amazing how inspired you can become when you allow yourself to open your heart and mind to this inspiring inner world.

Gratitude is the key that opens up the gateway of your heart and mind. It allows your love and inspirations to shine.

Whether you say your prayers of gratitude each day, give thanks before meals, write up your wish list, tune in to uplifting music, or spend some quiet time in contemplation or meditation, a little time spent partaking in a daily spiritual ritual of gratitude is incredibly nourishing for body, mind and spirit.

Affirmation:
I am forever grateful for my loving energy of life.

Be Grateful For Your Mental State
With gratitude, your mind becomes the most amazing place to explore.

How wonderful to have a mind of your own. Your mind makes up your private world, the secret part of yourself that often remains a mystery to others. Whether your mind becomes a friend or foe depends on how you master your perceptions, or how your unsettled mind's perceptions run you.

Your mind is like a garden. If you don't plant flowers in your mind's garden, you will forever be pulling weeds.

It is unwise to take your mind's powers for granted. You draw information in and send information out by your thoughts and ideas.

Your mind interprets, filters, and assimilates your concepts, strengths, fears, and desires. Being grateful for your mind's diverse, rich gifts helps it grow and expand.

Action steps:
Learn something new every day. Keep a book of inspiration nearby.

Affirmation:
I am grateful for my mind because it provides me with an ability to think for myself and serve others.

Be Grateful For Your Vocational State
Gratitude has the power to transform your vocation into a vacation.

Slipping into your cozy bed each night with a feeling that you have accomplished something worthwhile each day is something certainly rewarding. Feeling productive is one of the most uplifting feelings you can experience. It helps you sleep soundly and heal.

Being grateful for your present vocational state doesn't mean you must forever remain in your nine-to-five work role. Whether your vocation makes you a homemaker, a student, an athlete, or even a holidaymaker, it is important that you feel that you have been productive throughout your day's activities—no matter what the form. For example, if you love to fish, you might view a day of productivity to be a great day of fishing. If you are a business person, it may mean the opportunity to close some deals. If you are a homemaker, it could mean cooking dinner for your family. Ultimately, being grateful for your own form of productivity completes your package of life. Without gratitude, a great deal of fulfillment will be missing from your everyday existence.

Productivity provides you with a sense of purpose, achievement, and satisfaction.

Action steps:
Each morning, set yourself seven highest-priority action steps that will ensure your vocational productivity. Do these actions first, before any less-productive distractions arise. If you follow these seven action steps, then you will be certain to complete each day of the week with a sense of gratitude for what you have achieved, not to mention that your life is likely to make a quantum leap forward as well.

Affirmation:
I am grateful for the ability to feel productive and serve.

Be Grateful For Your Familial State
With gratitude, the entire world suddenly becomes your loving family.

Family means different things to different people. You have an immediate family, like your marriage partner, children, and parents, and you have friends who are involved in family structures of a more unusual kind. Your personal sense of family or close connection may even take the form of a pet or a distanced friend with whom you only communicate via email. You may even regard all those who reside in your community, city, or world as part of your extended family.

But even if you consider yourself a loner, you still will have closer or more distant connections to certain individuals, groups, or other structures (even if only in your fantasies). These connections can be intimate or less personal and may even consist of groups of people rather than individuals. Ultimately, you have a family.

Action steps:
Sometimes you may forget the role that others play (and have played) in making your life complete. So spend some time each day thinking of those whom you love, such as immediate family members or old friends. Recall what their presence on this planet (or past presence, if they have already left this planet) meant and still means to you, and how it has contributed to your fulfillment. Thinking grateful and loving thoughts about others will open up your heart and enrich your life.

Affirmation:
I am grateful for those whom I love and those who love me in return.

Be Grateful For Your Financial State
With gratitude, you may materialize more money than you even need.

Being grateful for your financial state can be a tricky "attitude of gratitude" to master because you may be constantly in the habit of affirming to yourself that you don't have enough money. Your money woes may be one of your biggest stress tests, and you may be facing financial shortfalls, or your finances or money management may be your constant concern or pressure.

You can become one of those who can truly say they are grateful for their financial state. The sooner you are grateful for whatever you have, the faster you will attract greater financial abundance. Your very thoughts, like *"I don't have enough money,"* can make your life a self-defeating prophecy. If your mind fills with angst over your financial situation, then you may miss receiving the many riches that surround you.

Action steps:
If you find yourself being too busy worrying about finances, or feel "less wealthy" rather than "more wealthy," then begin counting your blessings today and become grateful for what you have and for the money you are about to earn.

Affirmation:
I am grateful for the financial abundance that surrounds me and is available to me.

Be Grateful For Your Social State
With gratitude, every day becomes a socially fulfilling opportunity.

There's a certain reason for the saying "novelty breathes freshness into everyday life." Variety and change create more balance in life. Doing the same things repeatedly is like re-reading the same pages in the book of life, and you soon become bored. Getting out of your routine, meeting people, sharing ideas, and finding out what works or doesn't work for others and yourself, helps you expand.

Your social and leisure life is important because being with others gives you the chance to see your world through their eyes. Gratefully socializing helps you relax, regain enthusiasm and energy, and allows you to share quality time with others. Being grateful for the opportunity to share experiences, whether that takes the form of playing golf, taking a vacation, or nurturing and creating old and new friendships, is an important part of your everyday life. Of course, when you love your work as if it were play and love your vocation if it were your vacation, then you certainly have much for which to be grateful, and you become inspired at your work.

Action steps:
Go out of your way to plan "social days" in advance so you may enjoy the anticipation in this experience of gratitude. Be friendly and open to new people coming into your life, and go out of your way to develop friendships that will enrich your life. This may mean that you are not to wait for others to invite you somewhere, but that you are to take the initiative and organize get-togethers yourself. Make an effort every day, to expand your social network and connections. Making a phone call or sending a card to someone you would love to have as a friend can set all kinds of new social wheels spinning.

Affirmation:
My life is wonderful. I do what I love and I love what I do with those whom I love.

Be Grateful For Your Physical State
With gratitude, my body becomes both a temple and an amusement park.

The greatest art form that exists on this planet is your human body.

What a magnificently structured temple of sacred architecture your human-body form represents. But are you grateful for it? Sometimes you may be, but other times you may be taking your body for granted.

Instead of complaining about the shape of your body ("I'm too fat, too thin, too short, or too tall"), be grateful for your body. You may be spending a great deal of time in front of the mirror focusing on what you perceive to be the imperfections of your body rather than gratefully focusing on its beautiful or handsome perfections.

If you are consciously or unconsciously going out of your way to break down your magnificent body by smoking, eating poorly, not exercising, or burning the candle at both ends, then begin now to be grateful for your lovely body and for the multitude of powerful gifts it provides. This gratitude attitude can make the difference between experiencing wellness or illness. What you may term as "illness" may actually be your body's clever way of intuitively guiding you back to balance and more meaningful and grateful actions.

Action steps:
Be acutely aware of your body. Do not just expect it to maintain its own well-being without any contribution or effort on your part. Think of your body as a gift. It serves to bring you fulfillment in life. Tend to your body and take care of it, as you would tend to or take care of your garden.

Affirmation:
My incredible body is a created masterpiece, hand-signed by G.O.D.

♡♡♡

Dr. John F. Demartini is the founder of the Demartini Human Research and Education Foundation. He travels the world teaching and appearing on international radio and television shows. Dr. Demartini has been featured in newspapers and magazines throughout the world. As a private consultant, he has advised people from all walks of life.

Dr. Demartini has authored dozens of best-selling books.

www.drdemartini.com

Thank God My Father Died

BY DR. PAUL E. LANTHOIS

*How connecting with my father's spirit
helped me regain my own.*

I had a thriving business, a loving family, and was financially secure. Yet, I felt a sense of emptiness... a sense I was meant to do more with my life. My life was nice and comfortable, but I realized it had lost its spark, its passion, and its vitality. My life had lost its spirit.

On February 4, 2006, as I was driving to visit my ill father, I made the conscious decision to reclaim my spirit and live the type of life of which I had always dreamed. In the car, I decided after Dad passed on (which I thought would be sometime within the next two years), my family and I would sell everything and move to the other side of the country. What I was going to do, and how I was going to do it, I didn't know. All I knew is we had to move...

That visit to my father was the last time I saw him alive. Dad died two days later.

On February 6, 2006, while I was doing a consultation, I was interrupted by an urgent phone call: *"Dad's dead! He's here and he's dead. Dad's dead!"*

The sheer intensity and raw emotion in my brother's voice over the phone that day will be forever etched in my memory. My heart went out to my brother. I wished he weren't the one who had to experience the shock of finding Dad's lifeless body. I wished it had been me because I had been working in the health profession for fifteen years. At least I had some experience in dealing with the topic of death.

I quickly got into my car to meet my brother at the apartment where Dad was staying. Although Dad's death was hardly a surprise, it was still a huge shock. I thought it was going to happen someday soon, but now? As I was driving to Dad's apartment, an eerie calmness came over me. I recalled the thoughts I had two days earlier as I was driving along the same route. Taking a few deep breaths, I contemplated the impact of Dad's death. I realized the time for a major change in my life was now.

When I arrived at Dad's apartment, my brother and I sobbed and hugged each other so tightly, in the hope it would somehow ease the pain. It didn't.

I went into the small, dark, apartment where, on the bed, lay a lonely figure draped with a white sheet. It was surreal. I gathered myself by the side of the bed and finally mustered enough courage to lift the sheet. I hugged my dad's lifeless body, struggling to comprehend how my big, strong, wisecracking father could be reduced to this. He was so different without life coursing through his body… just an empty shell.

Refusing to give in to reality, I even checked Dad's vital signs, hoping for a flicker of life. But there was none. For the next thirty minutes, I hugged and looked at Dad, trying to take in as much information about him as possible, to ensure I would not forget him.

After my father's funeral and after finalizing his affairs, I visited one of my mentors, Mardi, who does spiritual energy balancing. I told her I had no idea of any direction in my life, and all I knew was that I had to move to the other side of the country. Mardi said I would start to attract the people, places, events, and circumstances that would assist me in my journey. How right she was!

That night, I went to a health talk and began sharing my intention to move to the other side of Australia. There, I met an amazing nutritionist and author named Erica, who, by chance, used to live in the area to which I was moving. I was intrigued by this person as she seemed completely different from anyone I had met before, yet strangely familiar. I was certain I was meeting her for an important reason, especially when she revealed the translation of her surname meant 'angel.'

We shared stories of remarkably similar journeys in our lives. I was inspired by her stories of what it meant to be able to make a difference in other people's health on an international scale.

I returned to work with a renewed sense of vigor, buoyed by the knowledge I was somehow being guided in my journey.

Within two months, I had sold my practice to an exemplary young man and agreed to stay on for the following six months in a part-time capacity, assisting with the transition, as I waited for my children to finish their school year.

Around this time, I had become so focused on the changes in my life I forgot about my wife, Angela. She was understandably hesitant about our comfortable lifestyle being turned upside-down in the selfish pursuit of my dream. Our marriage had been so strong, now, for the first time, it too was uncertain. Just the thought of this sent my world into a spin.

I didn't know what to do, so I went for a walk in nature to clear my head and get some sort of perspective on my life. I rested on a rock, where I realized that the only person in the world who I really wanted to talk to about this was Dad. This triggered an expression of grief so raw it felt exactly like when I was crying by my father's gravesite. My crying continued unabated for the next fifteen minutes. I was at my lowest ebb. I looked to the heavens and surrendered.

"I give up. What in the ... should I do now?" I screamed at the top of my lungs until there was no more grief, anger, and desperation inside of me.

I gathered myself and began the hike back out of the forest, thinking about how I longed to speak to Dad. I had walked approximately fifteen steps when I heard my father's voice over my right shoulder. *"You know, I am here if you need to talk."* My body tingled with goose bumps of exhilaration as tears of joy washed down my cheeks. *"You can write books and teach people how to regain their spirit. You can call it 'Teen Spirit.'"*

Instantly, a vision flashed in my mind of going on a book tour and giving presentations on health, energy, and life fulfillment to groups all over the world. This was accompanied by an amazing sense of euphoria for rediscovering some purpose in my life. I then thought to

myself, *"How do I go about writing a book?"* A picture
of Erica (the author I had met a few months earlier)
flashed into my mind.

My feelings intensified as I appreciated the synchronicity
of the recent events. The pieces of the puzzle were
starting to fit together. It was amazing. Within five
minutes of experiencing some of the most intense feelings
of grief I can ever recall, I was now feeling one of my
life's most amazing highs. I laughed at the inevitable ups
and downs of life I had long striven to avoid for the sake
of stability. The intensity of this experience really jolted
my senses, and I was now feeling alive like never before.

Later that afternoon, I tracked down Erica's number and
plucked up the courage to call her. She not only supported
my book idea, but also actively encouraged me to make a
difference to others with this book. She passed on a lot of
what she had learned throughout her writing journey and
recommended I go to a writing conference in Hawaii to
fast track my learning.

I began doing a lot of research and writing in my spare
time, as I completed my work commitments amidst
organizing our belongings. After Christmas, 2006, my
family and I traveled to our new home, 5000 kilometers
away in Queensland. Motivated by my life's purpose, I
continued writing and decided to go to the writer's
seminar in Hawaii.

During this conference, I lost my way around the hotel
and unintentionally ended up at a presentation by one of
the people featured on The Secret, Lisa Nichols. Towards
the end of her presentation, Lisa mentioned one of her
teen support programs called 'Teen Spirit...' Recognizing
my father's very own words, my ears pricked up as I

realized I was again being guided. As Lisa walked off the stage, she pointed to me and mouthed, *"I'll speak to you soon."*

People sitting adjacent to me turned to me saying, *"Did you see that? Was she talking to you? What do you have to talk about?"* The hairs on the back of my neck were again on end as I knew I had to go and speak to her to find out about this program.

After speaking with Lisa about Teen Spirit, I became quite emotional, so I walked out to the hotel foyer where I took in the incredible view of the ocean. There, I heard that same voice in my head …it was Dad again. *"Thanks for remembering, mate,"* he said. *"I…I'm proud of you."*

For the next forty-five minutes, an enormous feeling of love overwhelmed me. I cried with joy as it felt like everyone in the world was hugging me, saying, *"I love you."* Staying connected to this feeling, I became aware that part of Dad's purpose in his life was to help me become inspired about health. *"You went through all of that to help me?!"* I exclaimed, while recalling the suffering he went through in the second half of his life. I felt so humble.

I resolved, if Dad went through this to help me find my inspiration, nothing was going to stop me from helping others regain their energy and spirit. I strode with an air of confidence into my meetings with the interested publishers and agents. For the first time in my life, I was completely clear and assured about who I really was as a person —and what my purpose in life was.

My father, in his passing, became my ultimate spiritual guide —leading me through the most incredible range of the real part of them. I now see my spirit as a real part of me.

I am sharing this story to help other people who may be facing a similar situation in their lives. Yes, you will probably be experiencing some pain, sadness, and desperation as you face the mortality of a loved one. But I say this to you with the utmost conviction and clarity because I know deep inside that this is the truth. Amidst this suffering, there is joy, happiness, peace, and contentment.

How do you find these gifts amidst your despair?

Start to look for them. Start by interpreting your current events in a different way. Look at them with a different perspective and pay attention to your emotions. Use your emotions as a guide. As you explore different interpretations of your circumstances, pay attention to interpretations which make you feel better.

If you're feeling bad, that is your heart and soul saying there is another way of looking at things. It's your body telling you to look deeper. The stronger the pain, the more important it is to delve deeper. Your body will let you know with bursts of positive emotions when you have found these gifts amidst your sorrow. As a result of the beautiful gifts that have arisen from my wonderful father's death, I can say from deep in my heart ...

"Thank God my dad died."

♡♡♡

Dr. Paul Lanthois is a Doctor of Chiropractic with over 25 years of experience, Pain Expert and Author of "Healthy Pain: Winning The Pain Game" who has become a leading expert specializing in what is fast becoming the new standard for pain relief.

Having successfully overcome the debilitating pain of migraines and a fractured spine in his youth and the emotional pain of his father's death as an adult, Dr. Lanthois discovered that many times the most effective pain relief is to not to medicate the pain or even treat your pain.

Instead, Dr. Lanthois recommends you to learn to use your pains to see your bigger health picture, helping you heal your life and the true cause of your pain at the same time.

Married with three children, Dr. Lanthois currently spends his time in private practice in Queensland, Australia and developing online health support tools and advice for those wanting to heal the cause of their pain.

www.BeHealthyChiropractic.com.au
www.YourHealthyPain.com

Thank God I Became Chronically Ill

BY DR. PHILIP AGRIOS

A shocking jolt in my neck woke me from a deep sleep as though lightning bolts of pain from a stormy night were shooting down my arms into my hands. It's that severe pain that stops you from speaking as you wait for it to be over.

As I lay there for a few minutes and composed myself, I rolled out of bed as best I could without putting any weight on my hands. As my feet touched the cold wooden floor, I attempted to walk to the bathroom.

It was one of those nights where even my feet were affected. As I placed weight on one side of my foot, I quickly used the other to limit the amount of time I would spend touching the ground. It looked and felt like I was walking on glass.

As I sat to give my feet a rest, I caught myself staring into the darkness. This was my life now.

A few months later, I found myself staring again– but this time it wasn't into the darkness. It was a cold day in

January and I was staring at the outside lock to what was my office. It was the last time I would lock that door.

"How did this happen? This practice was my baby?" I whispered to myself.

When I opened those doors as a first-time practicing chiropractic physician, I had only one suite. But my practice expanded over the next few years to encompass the entire left side of the building, growing into a 2700 square foot clinic that housed medical doctors, physical therapists, nutritionists and other health professionals. It was a thriving practice that helped so many patients.

Now, with a January wind hitting my back, I was closing the doors for good.

I'd been diagnosed as having what is known as "thoracic outlet syndrome" on both sides of my neck. It happens because of an inadequate passageway through an area between the base of the neck and the armpit causing compression of nerves and blood vessels. I also had carpal tunnel syndrome in both hands. Since chiropractic, physical therapy and exercise failed, I was told my only option was surgery, which did not have a high success rate.

I'd been told by three physicians that I would never practice again. It felt like one of my kids just died. I felt powerless to cure myself, and I felt that I had let down the community, my patients, and my family. I was at rock bottom.

To make matters worse, I had neglected my health and my family as events years prior took a toll on me. A volatile marriage, the death of my father from brain cancer which subsequently caused me to become the primary caretaker for my ailing mother, and a three-year legal battle that dismantled my multi-discipline practice.

I broke down—mentally, physically and spiritually. I was told I was clinically depressed.

At this extreme low, I eventually realized that there had to be some type of gift that I would be given from all this– to have so much chaos and to lose so much—there must be a purpose. I knew this had to be so from other successful people's biographies. Many of them took devastating situations and used them to not only better themselves but others.

I began searching for answers, at first by meditating, listening to motivational speakers, and praying. However, it only helped for a little while. An intense and addicting roller coaster of emotions would consume me, causing me to flip flop between inspiration and desperation.

One day as I was walking down my basement steps, I heard physicist Dr. Michio Kaku talk about the Theory of Everything on the Science Channel. I never heard about it before, and I absorbed every word. It was at that moment, something clicked.

Years before, I had done a lot of thinking about how the universe worked and I saw a lot of correlations between the laws of nature and human behavior. When I heard Dr. Kaku that day, I knew I was onto something.

I then immersed myself in study, delving into physics, math and all of the sciences to come to a deeper understanding of the universe and the correlation to my work.

If I was going to find the gift within losing my practice, it would start here. I now had the time. To keep my sanity, I started to write about suffering, desperately looking for an answer within. All of this had to be for a reason.

It was a slow process but every month, every experience gained me insight. I started to observe myself re-creating old limiting patterns into my present day life, that had existed from years past. I'd long been aware that my discipline was lacking—but now I noticed how my physical disability gave me excuses to fester this behavior.

What's more important, my disability gave me the ability to be still, to show me the tugging battle that was raging within my being. By becoming aware, it influenced me to start changing my life, and the reason was I wanted to, not because I had to.

I went on to observe how and why I was creating my illness.

By using my newly found insights, I started re-educating my body's reaction to stress. I started to feel healthier, stronger and I felt I had a purpose again. I was able to start practicing and helping people once more.

Although I continued to be faced with challenges—the passing of my mom, personal difficulties with my children, a divorce, and problems with my current place of employment, something was different. This time, I was not the same doctor nor the same person. This time, I knew there was a light at the end of the tunnel. And it was screaming, *"Your work is not complete!"*

I realized that the world we live in is filled with dichotomies: up-down, left-right, in-out, yin-yang, good-bad—and I had a choice of whether to see something as good or bad, as a benefit or a detriment. Thus, I was able to turn old thinking into opportunities. The path which the universe had laid out before me years prior, was illuminated now.

I dove more into my own behavior and correlated it with my patients' patterns. It was then one day on my living room floor that I discovered that there are specific archetypal patterns of stress reactions, and that we all tend to fall into one of these categories.

My living room floor discovery expanded into a program that enabled me to build a new type of practice empowering chronically ill patients to take back control of their health and their lives.

The anger, frustrations and despair I had felt allowed me to go within for the answers to not only healing myself, but in assisting others to heal.

Being swallowed up into that deep, dark place of murky despair, enabled me to resurface with inspired clarity— the answers were within me and not outside.

By trusting the universe and allowing my new destiny to unfold, I was able to access and mold a unique tool to guide others back to health. Thank God I became chronically ill!

♡♡♡

Dr. Philip Agrios, *DC, DACBSP, D.PSc is an integrative wellness practitioner, personal coach, speaker, author and the creator of Life's One Law. His background is a doctor of chiropractic with specialized training in functional endocrinology, functional neurology and a board certified chiropractic sports physician. He uses nutrition, personal coaching, and holistic treatments to help chronically ill patients take back control of their health and their life. He specializes in autoimmune conditions.*

http://www.healthswitchwellness.com/

Thank God My Daughter Committed Suicide

BY JENETTA BARRY

*T*here were several occasions after Jenny, my daughter, committed suicide where I contemplated killing myself. It was on the eve of the second anniversary of her death that I succumbed to a very dark moment in my life.

I had traveled to the UK with the intent to set up a light base there, from which to also conduct my business. As the dates for what would have been Jenny's 18th birthday, as well as the second anniversary of her death, drew closer and the winter began to close in, I slipped into my deepest and darkest place. I had organized to take a week off from working in order to visit my brother in Oxford, and some days beforehand, I found myself seriously preparing how to end my life.

As I planned this process through, I began to deeply understand the similarity between physical and emotional pain. Several years previously, while undergoing radiation treatment for cancer, I had hemorrhaged in the intestine. I remember getting to the point where the combination of pain and feeling seriously ill became too overwhelming to handle. It felt as though dying and being released from the pain was the only reasonable option.

Now with these circumstances, it felt as though I was operating with the same degree of pain, but on an emotional level. An emotional pain that was too overwhelming to cope with. I then realized that I might have an idea of the depth of emotional pain Jen, my daughter, must have felt for most of her life ...

"You've fucked up my life! You've fucked up my friendships!"

Jen's words rang in my ears as she stormed out to her bedroom situated on the other side of our house's inner courtyard. We had had an enormous argument, and I, as her Mom, had applied tough love to my 16-year old child.

Over a period of time, Jen had become more and more manipulative, using the threat of not coping with life and suicide to maneuver herself out of being responsible and accountable. This had resulted in her balking at standard house rules required for her safekeeping. I had written her a loving, but firm letter earlier in the day, indicating to her that challenging and breaking these rules was inappropriate and that it was vital for her well-being that she should conform. This had resulted in our argument, and now she was in her room packing her bags to leave home.

I attempted to distract myself by sending a cell phone text to a friend but finally with a feeling of immense unease, I went to check up on her. I walked into her bedroom, and saw that it had been trashed. Her belongings had been thrown everywhere.

The family dog was sitting at the end of the bed... Jenny was not there... I moved the curtain that separated her bedroom from her bathroom... And found her... hanging from her shower rail with a broken neck. I climbed onto the chair she had used to jump from and attempted to take her body weight off her neck, but I realized it was useless. I urgently called out to Nellie, our family housekeeper to fetch and bring a pair of scissors, and as I cut my beautiful daughter down from the necktie noose she had made, I found myself mentally, physically and emotionally distraught on many levels.

Thinking rapidly ... *"How do I revive her?"* ... *"Do I call someone for help or run down the road to find a neighbor?"* ... *"Do I stay and try to save her?"* ... Take action. Take action. Take action ... Which first?

I dashed to the phone and called a friend and with frantic calm, ran down the road to find at-home neighbors. In the meantime, Nellie had run to call another neighbor from the other end of our street and on my returning to the house, this neighbor was exiting Jenny's room. She was deeply distressed, shocked, and in fright. She shouted at me, asking what had happened because my daughter was dead. I knew then that there was nothing more I could do ... it was over. I collapsed in an anguished daze on the lawn outside the house, unable to move or take action anymore.

Part of me was desperate to bring Jenny back to life; the other part of me was filled with overwhelming relief that she was no longer able to hurt herself, that she was now 'safe' and no longer my responsibility. This had been her fourth attempt to kill herself, and now she had finally succeeded.

I abstractly observed people come and people go. I watched the mortuary men arrive with their van to prepare and take Jenny's body away. At one point (I have no recollection of doing it), when asked by the police what had happened, I apparently beat my hands on the garage wall and cried out that I had killed Jenny and that it was my fault she was dead.

A little later, a crisis volunteer approached me, and as she settled down on the grass to counsel me, I saw her name badge read, *"Jenny."* Even through my shock, my mind took note: *"What a coincidence!"*

The days that followed were combined with vivid accounts etched in my memory, together with happenings I inadvertently blanked out and had to be reminded about. We held a church memorial service for Jen, which was followed by a 'celebration of her life' ceremony held in a marquee in our garden.

As I finally accepted that Jen was dead, I pondered the fact that she had been our most celebrated child—the much-anticipated daughter after two boys. On her arrival, I felt blessed being able to experience that precious mom-daughter relationship.

Over the years and on the surface, Jenny appeared to be a mostly happy child with an engaging smile and an inquiring mind. From time to time, though, she displayed puzzling signs of irrationality and unreasonableness.

By way of example, when she was about 18 months old, she created quite a stir in our neighborhood. I had collected her from kindergarten one lunch time, and while easing the car back into traffic, for no apparent reason, she began to cry. During the fifteen-minute journey back to our house, her cries built up to a bloodcurdling crescendo, as if she was being seriously attacked. Neighbors ran out of their houses to assist, and once we had removed her from the car, she just lay screaming, prostate on the pavement. For a good half an hour, absolutely nothing would console her and only once she had become completely spent did her screams finally end. Within twenty minutes, she was back to her normal self, interacting as though nothing had happened.

On another occasion when she was four years old, she accidentally spilled a flask of very hot water over herself. Her shrieks of pain transformed into anguished screaming, not because she was burning, but because she didn't want to expose her nipples to everyone present.

When she was eight, her best friend's family had invited her to join them for a celebratory birthday dinner. At first, Jen assumed that she could go wearing a pair of jeans and a t-shirt. But because this was going to be held at an upscale restaurant, and Jenny was the only friend who had been invited, I took out her special occasion dress—a beautiful tartan from the UK. As we were getting ready to leave, she showed up wearing it with a large hole she'd cut right in the center so there would be no other choice but for her to go in her everyday clothes.

It came as a shock when shortly after she turned thirteen, Jenny claimed that she was the family outcast. She was convinced she had been swapped in the hospital as a baby because she felt she had never belonged to our family.

She also confessed to having secretly felt suicidal for most of her life, and that when she was about seven, she had once tried to choke herself to death with her hands whilst standing in front of her mirror. Friends and family were equally surprised with this revelation, as Jen mostly appeared to be a happy child.

As a teenager, after several suicide attempts and two sessions in rehab, she continued to battle with friends' verbal slights and their perceived insensitive actions, which had the capacity to shift her into a dark place emotionally. At this time her eating disorder kicked in, and overall her schoolwork took a nosedive, and it was very apparent that her self-worth and sense of purpose were severely compromised.

At 13, Jen was expelled from rehab hospital for "bad behavior" after attempting to overdose and cut her wrists in the gardens outside her ward. She and two other adolescent patients subsequently ran away into the streets of Johannesburg. We lost her for thirty hours straight, and I feared that we would never see or hear of her again. She was eventually found locked in a house not too far away from the place they had run away from. Those thirty very long hours felt like the end of the world. Nobody really knows what was happening deep inside her.

I once suggested to Jenny that she was taking life too seriously and that she should try to take her friends' actions more lightly and embrace these happenings as being a part of life and that she had the ability to choose to feel differently.

Her answer was, *"But Mum, everyone is presuming that I feel like everyone else. This is the way I feel, and it is very real to me. How and what everyone else feels and how they cope does not help me."*

Now it was I who nobody understood. I realized that everyone who knew me had no idea what depth of pain I was feeling. Instead, there was an air of acceptance from them, a silent expectation, a general message in body and word that after this amount of time, I should have suitably moved on. And it was this lack of understanding from the people around me that paralyzed me further with overwhelm.

Yes, at this second anniversary mark, my emotional pain barometer had plummeted to an all-time low.

While in this state, I had nonetheless planned to travel to take a week's break with my brother where he lived in Oxford. We had everything planned down to the detail of texting him from the train to let him know when I was close to arriving at the station.

But I had had a counter-plan—and this one I kept to myself. I had decided that living this emotional pain was more than I could bear and so I made a plan to end my life.

I'd found a town and bed and breakfast and train route in the opposite direction, but didn't book as I didn't want to leave a trail where my loved ones could find me. I wanted to go somewhere far away. I wanted to spare them ... I wanted to just disappear.

After Jen's death I had dealt with my marriage ending and my youngest daughter choosing to live with her Dad, and I had been trying with all my might to focus on picking up the millions of broken pieces that now made up my life, and place them together to live a 'normal' life once again. I'd gotten to a point where I believed it was an impossible task. Part of my overwhelm was that I had not anticipated a nosedive in my grieving, two years on. It was daunting. Feeling emotionally isolated and alone, my days became blurred and I shuffled through the hours like an automated puppet.

On the eve of my departure while packing my bags, I unexpectedly received a phone call from my brother. For some reason, he chose to call me the night before to confirm my arrival time. It was this phone call that kicked me out of my initial focus and which enabled me to process that these challenging circumstances could change. I re-planned my train route and arrived safely at my brother's flat.

A few days later while sitting in meditation, I began observing the emotional pain that had me almost leave this world. In the flash of a moment, I gained deeper clarity ... a startling understanding of the reasonableness of why Jen had killed herself. Even though in my logical mind I could acknowledge the unreasonableness by my and society's judgment of her killing herself, I equally felt a heart-opening understanding of the unreasonableness, for Jenny, of living a long life. I was able to understand that Jenny's uniqueness in deciding to leave this planet was a reasonable decision for her and that she had her own unique reasons.

Post-Jenny and right up to and beyond this lowest point, I had spent much time working on myself through meditating, facilitating intuitive workshops and at the same time, spending time Equilibrating my deep grief and loss. I consistently worked through a fourteen column Equilibrating chart about my memory of Jenny, which opened up a deeper understanding of that memory. This balancing process was hard work. I called it my daily mental, emotional and spiritual gym. Some days it felt impossible and on other days it flowed. I was driven by the determination that I just wasn't going to live the rest of my life trapped in a deep black imprisoning emotional hole.

With time, I noticed that my reaction to overwhelming situations shifted in big ways. I found that whenever challenged, I was able to more spontaneously speak from my heart ... to unearth a wisdom within me I had known was there before but could not quite fathom and which now naturally flowed out from me from deep within my soul. I became able to shift the story I had in my head that my life was dreadful—as much as Jenny's death has been a deep loss, it has also led me to live my life on purpose, something I had been searching to do for all my adult years.

With new clarity, I saw that Jen danced to the beat of her own drum and that leaving the planet was about transforming into something else. That seemingly coincidental happening with a social worker named 'Jenny' on my lawn was an initial example of my experiencing her in many new ways. I had always understood and wanted to believe in the connection with loved ones after they die. Since Jenny's passing, both myself and others have received so many lucid dreams, significant numbers, unusual rainbows at poignant times and other signs of connection that my faith in the universe and it's workings has stepped into a place of knowing. I now understand that her energy had never left but had re-formed in new ways.

As I sit at my desk today writing this heartfelt story, I acknowledge that working through the loss of my child is and always will be a lifetime process. At the same time, I am equally as thankful for the powerful once hidden gifts that I now have and work with in my life BECAUSE of this loss. Every day I wake up with a sense of purpose—

living my life on purpose—assisting people around the globe to work through their challenges and traumas with the application of Equilibration and I am deeply grateful for the legacy that all this will leave behind long after I am gone ...

♡♡♡

Jenetta Barry, Vice President of Sales and Marketing at ThankGodi.com, has spent over a decade as a grief and trauma specialist and is a world authority on Equilibration. After overcoming the traumatic suicide of her 16-year old daughter, Jenny, Jenetta authored "Full-Circle Rainbow" and was featured in Sarie Magazine.

Jenetta has consulted to world-leading corporations— including Avon (Justine), Bernina, Swissgarde and Tupperware Southern and East Africa—delivering inspirational speeches and keynoting at life-shifting events.

Subsequent to being diagnosed with uterine cancer, Jenetta expanded her studies by further questioning and researching standard methods of motivation. This shifted her focus to creating self-mastery techniques which in more recent years has seen her training and working with Dr. John Demartini and presenting alongside ThankGodi's CEO, John Castagnini.

Jenetta was featured in "Parents Magazine" for her work in Kenya, where she assisted the bereaved and injured in the Westgate Terrorist Attack in Nairobi and while there, keynoted for the American Women's Association.

She has been a regular featured guest on M-Net TV, is a published author in the #1 Amazon bestselling "Thank God I" series and is also author of the handbook, "A Handful of Keys for Grief Relief."

She is Mom to Stuart, Neil, (Jenny) and Catherine, as well as Gran to granddaughters Bella, Malaika, and Alexa.

Thank God I Experienced the Heaven and Hell of Fame

BY JIM LEYRITZ

*O*ne day, a single heart-wrenching event abruptly ended my very successful life as I had known it. In one shattering split-second, I turned from being a national sports celebrity, to fighting for my survival–and it literally became a fight for my life.

Millions of boys dream of being the guy who hits an historic home run.

I hit the home run that won the N.Y. Yankees the World Series for the first time in eighteen years, which in turn launched the N.Y. Yankee Dynasty into the 1990's.

My name is Jim Leyritz and I had a ten-year career as a major league ballplayer. My "claim to fame" was for my multiple playoff and World Series home runs.

I was one of those fortunate people, who had their lifetime moment in the sun. I went up against the best in the world in my field, and in the biggest game in sports I slammed the ball over the fence, under ultimate pressure. The face of fame has such irresistible allure– multimillion dollar contracts, parties with top celebrities, top media attention. The world was indeed my oyster.

Little did I know at the time that this same fame would soon send me crashing down to the point where I was fighting for my freedom, fighting for my life.

It started with a crash. After the impact and screeching, the two cars came to a rest. I exited my car and ran back down the street to the intersection where the collision had taken place. The other driver was a woman, and looking at the tiny blood drops rolling down her face made me realize that this wasn't just another accident. Someone else was standing over her and was trying to talk to her. I knew then that I had to go back to my car and get my phone and call someone to let them know that I was lucky to be alive.

It was after I came back to the scene and a police officer said, *"Stand here,"* that things began to take on nightmare proportions.

I was certain that the other driver had very clearly run the light and that she had hit my car. But as I stood watching and waiting, another officer informed me that a witness who had been driving behind the woman's car thought that her light had been green.

The other driver was unconscious and not breathing well. The ambulance paramedics were there and working flat out to save her.

Then I found out that the other driver had died!

I was distraught that a valuable life had been lost.

And with that turn of events, this night changed my life, my family's life, and the other woman and her family's lives forever.

That night was December 28, 2007, at 3:05 am.

The evening had started out as a happy, relaxed and loving celebration of my forty-fourth birthday. My three sons and I had been out to dinner and as I finished opening their presents, I received a call from a group of friends suggesting we meet up for birthday celebration drinks.

I dropped the boys off at their mom's house for the night and headed off to the Blue Martini. The level of anticipation there was high, filled with excited talk about our group heading to the Bahamas the next morning to celebrate the New Year. Slow service saw us moving to another venue and eventually, around 3:00 am, I decided it was time to get a couple of hours' sleep before picking up my sons to take them home with me again.

A young man who had come with my friends, hitched a ride home with me since it was on my way. Within minutes of leaving the carpark, everything came to a crashing halt at an intersection we were entering.

A car came flying through on their red light. Before we could use our brakes or react, there was that ear-splitting clash of metal as our two cars collided.

I had no idea that my nightmare had only just begun.

Three very long years later, I was finally standing in front of a jury of six people and was still waiting for a verdict on the charges of either DUI (driver under influence) manslaughter with the prospect of spending the next fifteen years of my life in jail, or just being sentenced with a simple charge of DUI.

The accident had become a national media story—I had gone from hero to zero in an instant.

My heart was pounding. We had fought for so long to prove that I had not been responsible for what had happened, and soon, either one or two words were going to decide my future forever.

Shortly after the accident, I had found out that I actually knew the other driver. She had just been served divorce papers by her husband– the papers were found in the car with her– and she had been drinking and was texting as she was driving.

None of this, however, was admissible as evidence— Florida had just enacted an anti "victim bashing" law, which meant that my case rested on a technicality– was the light red or green?

On my side, I had admitted from the outset that, yes, I'd been drinking and driving. I was adamant, however, that that was the only charge I was prepared to accept.

Eventually, my attorney tried to urge me to take a plea of a lesser charge, but I would not agree to take the easy way out. I was determined to clear my name. I knew from deep in my heart that it was the only way to handle this whole ordeal.

During those three years of waiting for trial, I found myself stepping stronger into my faith and I rededicated my life to God. I stood firm that He was in control of everything that was happening in my life. From the start, He had been giving me guiding signs confirming that I must not admit to doing something I did not do.

The plea I was being urged to take, would have not given me any time in jail, yet it would have left me with a charge of felony and probation for ten years.

I had waited three years to hear those two words–"not guilty"–and I was adamant that I was not going to accept anything less than that. I told my attorney that I trusted that the truth would come out in court.

Even though the state continued issuing delays, I doggedly continued fighting, despite the pain it was causing both families. I just knew that coming through would make a difference to all involved. It took forever to push to finally be in front of a jury.

Through all this time, I noticed how in some strange way, this horrible situation was producing positive steps for the future of our family.

During this time, my mom had stayed with me helping me with the boys. The whole ordeal brought us very close together– I had been awarded custody and had recently quit my baseball career to be a full-time dad. My 12-year-old held me for three nights in the beginning–"Daddy, you're ok ... you're here ... you're alive ... did you have your seatbelt on?" And through the pain of possibly losing their dad for fifteen years, the boys started attending church regularly. My mom through watching me go through all of this had brought God back into her life and had been saved again.

As you can imagine, money was an issue. Despite having made 10 million dollars over eleven years, I had spent all of my earnings on getting custody of my children. A Major League Baseball group called BAT (Baseball Assistance Team) sent a representative to look at the details of my case to see if they could help the boys and me out financially. I'd been using all of my own money to hire an attorney to defend me. After looking at all the evidence and depositions, he saw that I was being wrongly accused and gave the board permission to grant me whatever money the boys and I needed, as long as it wasn't used for the case. Another prayer had been answered.

I had heard that the State attorney had taken the case because they wanted the publicity for their campaign to become a Judge. I guess there's nothing better than taking down an infamous N.Y. Yankee legend to boost one's career. I Thank God I had the faith to not give in and to believe that, as the Scripture says, *"The truth will set you free."*

Now finally, it was Friday, November 20, 2010, and the trial was nearly over.

The jury had left the courtroom. We waited and waited. My whole life hung, suspended in that wait. Then the judge called them back in. At last I would know.

"Have you reached a decision?" the judge asked.

The jury foreman said: *"No, your honor, we have one person who is undecided."*

They were instructed to go home and sleep on it and deliver their verdict the next morning.

This was beyond painful. We didn't know what the juror was unsure of. Was it the manslaughter or was it the simple DUI? As you can imagine, my family couldn't sleep worrying what their undecidedness could be. This guided Michelle (my fiancé), mom and my kids to pray that night—not to be free or anything direct–just to affirm that God would lead the jury to come to a fair and just decision.

On talking it through, we felt that enough evidence had been given to clear me of the Manslaughter charges.

That bonding with my family that night is something I would never want to change. Without this adversity, we would never have experienced that precious gift of bonding and love in that deeply meaningful and unique way.

Returning for the verdict the following day tested us even further in practicing patience in faith. The jury was still at a stalemate and they were instructed to remain together until a decision was reached.

We left to go next door and have a coffee. Finally, while talking to my pastor for reassurance on the phone, they called us back in—the jury had reached a decision.

As we walked back, my nerves really started to take over with so many thoughts going through my mind. Then I remembered what Pastor Troy had said: *"No matter what, God is a fair and just God. You must have faith in that."*

I walked back to the chair I had been sitting in for twenty-one days.

Brian, the court foreman, stood up to read the verdict. I reached into my bag and held my Bible in one hand and a picture of my children in the other.

My heart was racing almost as much as my mind. As he began speaking, the officer standing next to me put handcuffs on my one arm. My heart sunk as this seemed to indicate I was in trouble, but as she put them on, she reassuringly said, *"It's ok, they'll be off in a minute."*

I wondered what she knew.

–And then I heard the words: *"Guilty on the lesser charge of DUI first time offense."* I didn't know what that meant. I looked at my attorney and he assured me that this was good. A slight "yes" erupted from my side of the courtroom.

Those few seconds seemed like a lifetime.

The stress and the pain all of these families had been through was finally over. I was later sentenced to one year probation and a $500 fine.

The lessons I learned through all this have changed my life and made me a better man than I ever could imagine.

Like a boy with a new toy, the allure of fame had me feel, at times, foolishly invincible. It was my fame that had put me through hell. At the same time, in going through hell, I discovered heaven in my faith.

I pray every day for the girl who passed away and her family. I also pray that as my trial and struggles were so public, that other people learn from my experience. I live now in California with my three sons who are with me full time. I have a beautiful new wife. She has two little girls. I am working for the L.A. Angels Radio Station, and my broadcasting career is finally moving forward again.

Had I not been part of that tragic night, I might still take my fame and the responsibilities that come along with it for granted. Now I take nothing for granted. I appreciate and am filled with gratitude for all that comes my way, the challenges included.

I learned that there is a fine balance in life, where challenges and achievements are important co-ingredients in the subtle mix to becoming and being successful.

My accident on December 28, 2007, has, without a doubt, turned my life around for the better.

♡♡♡

Jim Leyritz is a former MLB catcher/infielder/designated hitter and World Series champion with the New York Yankees (1990–1996, 1999–2000). "The King" is best known for hitting numerous post-season, playoff, and World Series home runs that either won, tied or changed the momentum of several series.

James Joseph Leyritz was born December 27, 1963, in Lakewood, Ohio, the youngest of three children. He attended Turpin High School in Cincinnati, Ohio and the University of Kentucky. Jim began attracting the attention of professional scouts in high school and despite never having been drafted, was signed as an amateur free agent by the New York Yankees in 1985.

Thank God My Mom Died

BY JOHN CASTAGNINI

"That's it! She's gone! It's over!"
"I allowed those doctors to kill her ... I didn't do enough!"
It was murder, and her blood was on my hands.
"I could've, should've ..."
It was all my fault!

J anuary 9, 2005–the date is engraved in my bones. It's the day my mom, Lorraine Castagnini, left this world at age fifty-six. I remember dropping the phone and crushing my ears with my hands trying to squeeze the news of her death out of my head.

My mom was a lot more than just my mom. My mom was my rock. She really knew how to walk the line between being my mom and my best friend. When I moved away to California, I called her pretty much every day simply because I loved to. I mean, I drove her nuts, I was an insane teenage boy, but there was nothing, absolutely nothing I would not talk to her about, and I shared it all.

My mom loved being a mom more than she loved anything else. Many of my friends during my childhood didn't have close relationships with their own mothers, so my mom became the neighborhood mom. This petite Italian woman from Brooklyn really enjoyed chasing little boys around the kitchen table with a wooden pasta spoon as much as she loved her coffee and cigarettes.

Mom truly knew me in many ways better than I knew myself. She would often quote the serenity prayer to me:

"God grant me the serenity to accept the things I cannot change, the courage to change the things I can, and the wisdom to know the difference."

After her death, a tortuous new mantra took over my mind: *"I tried so hard, but obviously not hard enough, to help you discover your road back to health."*

For the final five months that my mom was on this earth, we were at extreme odds. I had recently left my childhood sweetheart, in essence, my mom's only daughter.

The evening before Mom died, I didn't even see her as my mom anymore. *"That's not her,"* I told myself, *"she looks like a crack addict,"* She looked like someone who was going to die. Five hours later, she had a heart attack and was gone.

For years, I'd fought with my father over what the doctors were prescribing for her. Having trained as a chiropractor, I knew that their diagnoses and pills were all wrong. They kept diagnosing her "disease" after "disease" while prescribing whatever would put her into a stupor, anything to numb the pain, never addressing the cause. My father refused to listen to me, and I was stuck with questioning what to do. This went on for years.

Had I tuned out her cries for help? She'd been silently screaming, begging for something I failed to give her. In my work, I'd been fighting furiously to hear people's internal challenges. Yet, I'd neglected to hear the most valuable person in my universe.

"Please someone cut off my head," I couldn't stop obsessing. I staggered under the grief, as if I had control of the death card. Consumed, confused, and alone, the little boy inside me wanted his mommy.

For the thirteen years before my mom passed, I'd devoted my professional life to helping people overcome traumas and tragedies. Death of a loved one, rape, divorce, molestation—my clients had been through it all—and I helped them find their silver linings. As impossible as it seemed, I knew that it was my time to work on myself.

I pretty much isolated myself and looked inward. With pen and paper, I started listing each challenge that I felt with my mom's passing—and there were a ton of them. As difficult as it was, I began putting into writing how each of these painful challenges might serve me in my life.

I also listed each quality my mom had represented to me—her nurturing and friendship, her humor and empathy, her unconditional love for me. According to the first law of thermodynamics—the law of conservation of energy—energy and matter are neither created nor destroyed, but only change forms. All of us are this energy transforming. Logically, it made complete sense that I could find my mom's qualities in other forms in the people around me—but how?

Each time I looked for the transformation, my mind and my heart would go into a panic. I so wanted to hold on to the identity of a little boy grieving over the loss of his mom. The worst part of it was I missed my mom's support. Where was this unconditional love now? Who would mother me now? What were the advantages of being separated from my mom's unconditional love? Now, I would have to find and trust the inner voice inside of me.

The tug of war raging inside me threatened to pull me into a bottomless pit. The universe had thrown me onto my ultimate crossroad. Either I'd find the perfect balance in my mom's passing, or I'd have to realize that what I'd been teaching my clients was bullshit.

Then one day while working it through with pen and paper, I found myself feeling lighter, as if something had let go, something had shifted inside. I really didn't know what happened. I just felt inside that something was ok. Basking in this new inner peace, I put down my pen to go to a restaurant for dinner. My girlfriend came with me.

While we were in the parking lot, a woman walked by and caught my attention. Our eyes locked and she said "hello" with her smile. I introduced myself and asked her name.

"Lorraine," she responded.

Lorraine! Same name as my mom, and not exactly the most common name. I asked Lorraine where she was from.

"Brooklyn," she replied, which was where my mom was from. I was highly suspicious at the coincidence, so I asked Lorraine her age.

This Lorraine was fifty-six years old—my mom's age when she died. This Lorraine was holding a cup of coffee in one hand and a cigarette in the other—my mom loved those damn cigarettes!

It felt like there was no separation between me and the new Lorraine—or anyone or anything else for that matter. It felt like I was floating along with everyone and everything else, like there was a light beam connecting us all. I felt a calm inner knowing inside.

I whispered to my girlfriend, *"I guarantee this Lorraine's birthday is January ninth"*– the same day my mom had passed.

The woman stared through my eyes with laser focus when I asked when her birthday was.

"January ninth," she shouted, *"Why?"*

Then she got into a waiting car and was driven away. It seemed like she'd disappeared, like a ghost.

Was this a living breathing confirmation that mom was still around somewhere?

What are the chances of meeting another 56-year-old Lorraine from Brooklyn whose birthday would be on my mom's death day? And what made me know and voice her birthday in advance?

Had I transcended the space-time illusion and experienced the eternal present?

Ever since I was a teenager, my mind was obsessed with understanding life and death. The greatest tragedy of my life, the death of my mother, gave to me the greatest gift possible—I transcended the illusion that there is any separation between life and death. In that moment, life and death became one. We are all both dead and alive in the eternal present. My mother's death helped me overcome any fear of death. Talk about transformation–wow!

In thanking my mom for opening my eyes to a greater understanding of the Grand Organized Design, I constructed a beautiful scrapbook of our life together. It began with a few simple pictures and became a year of daily meditation in scrapbook building. I honored our precious moments and all she ever was to me.

I stopped beating myself up and acknowledged that during her last illness I visited her almost daily–I'd even chosen to live four blocks away from her. After her passing, I found I had a more profound relationship with her. I listened in ways I couldn't before. I heard my mom, and we both discovered a new "one another," closer and deeper in our communication. Before, there was my mom; now, there is my mom and her free soul guiding my spirit. I understood this beautiful woman came to this planet to be a mother. She wanted to die a mother. Her boys were turning into men, and dying was how she let go. She couldn't let go and stay here with us. She had to leave for us to really let go and think for ourselves.

This woman who birthed me gave me a second life in her dying. Since her death, I try to listen more closely and open my heart wider to others, and myself, just the way she lived.

"Mom, I understand it was your time to leave. I understand and honor your freedom to change. I realize that no matter how hard I would have tried to shift our

roles a bit, and tell you what I think you should do, you wanted to live and die 'The Mother.' "

"Thank you for the gift of serenity for that which I cannot change. God knows, no one was going to change you! By my facing this great challenge of your leaving so young and so suddenly, you instilled in me the courage to discover and change the only thing I can change: my own mind. Thank you for the courage to share our story. I will cherish this courage with every breath until my very last. Yes, Mom, when you left I was lost, but thanks to you, I now am found I was blind, but now I see. Mom, you were one powerful little woman in your life–and even more powerful now."

♡♡♡

John Castagnini created the ThankGodi series in 2006. In this, he was inspired by the power of appreciation and the untimely death of his Mom, Lorraine Castagnini.

John's work has been covered on ABC-TV, in The Huffington Post, and in the Hollywood film, Discover The Gift, where John was featured along with Rev. Michael Beckwith, Marianne Williamson, and the Dalai Lama. John has authored dozens of industry leading consciousness development products, written over 2000 poems, co-authored the World Class Achievement Series with New York Yankee legend, Jim Leyritz and is CEO of ThankGodi.com. John attended chiropractic school, holds a BA in biology, and is an avid student of the martial arts. He held events in the 1990's with Dr. Wayne Dyer and Dr. John Demartini.

Thank God I Was a Runaway Child

BY JOHN JOSEPH

*M*y name is John Joseph. My father was an alcoholic prizefighter, and as a result of his violence, our family was broken up in 1967 where, at the age of five, myself along with my two brothers, were placed into foster care in New York State. We ended up in a house of horrors on Long Island where for almost seven years, we were starved as well as physically, emotionally and sexually abused. We had to steal just to put any food in our stomachs. Our foster parents told us constantly that no one loved us and that we should be thankful that they took us in. We were also tormented in the neighborhood and at school because we were the foster kids who lived in the "crazy house" with the "crazy people."

After the foster home was shut down by the State and all the foster kids removed (six in total), we were bounced around to other foster homes and group homes. Finally, in 1977, at the age of fourteen, I'd had all I could stand of the State's idea of childcare, and I ran away from St. John's Home for Boys in Rockaway Beach, ending up on the mean streets of New York City.

I swore daily I would be someone, be something, so I could throw it back in the faces of the people who turned their backs on me. Then I could say, *"See, look what you didn't want anything to do with. Look who I am now."* I had so much anger and hatred toward the world for what was done to me and I really resented my mother for never taking us back. I lashed out at everyone. I was as violent as they came and in NYC in those days, as a kid on the streets, you had to be. I was a heroin mule, a hustler, a scammer, a drug dealer, a drug user and a thief. I was shot, stabbed and I did a lot of things I'm not proud of, but that I had to do just to survive.

Just before my sixteenth birthday, after almost two years on the streets and several criminal cases, I was incarcerated for 21 months in some of the worst juvenile detention centers New York had to offer. The violent behavior continued as you had to fight every day in those places and I was labeled by psychiatrists as a time bomb waiting to go off.

After lock up, I caught another case as I went back to what I knew, hustling and dealing drugs. I was offered jail or the military. I joined the Navy.

Initially I thrived in the military, and I thought everything was going well, but the problem was I never faced the demons of my childhood. I never dealt with the ticking time bomb that was inside of me. I used alcohol and drugs to self-medicate. I smuggled drugs aboard my ship and sold drugs in Norfolk while wearing the U.S. Navy uniform. I sold drugs to an undercover officer and was arrested. Then I beat someone up on my ship to the point he was in intensive care. That's when I went AWOL.

I was on the streets again with warrants and no place to turn. I was so lost. I didn't know where to turn. I prayed to God to help show me the way. Direct me. Take away the pain I had inside of me.

My prayers were answered.

While I was in Norfolk, I met a musical group called the "Bad Brains." They talked of love and peace and were surrounded by positive people who were into yoga, meditation, and vegetarianism. I ran into them again in NYC while I was AWOL and we developed a very close bond. They even offered me a job as their roadie and I took it, seeing it as a blessing to be surrounded by such amazing people every day. The Bad Brains and their entourage became my family. We prayed, talked and had great times traveling around the country living out our dreams.

I gave up drugs, meat eating, and drinking. I got into hathayoga and even got a side job at a health food store in NYC. Great right? All the food I could eat. My life was truly amazing at that point. I eventually joined my own group called, The CroMags, and we put out records, toured, and were even filmed in a Hollywood movie with the famous producer of "Taxi Driver" and "Close Encounters ..." Julia Phillips.

I had such a great spiritual foundation. It was then that I joined the Hare Krishna religion and lived as a monk for two years; only to be betrayed by them as I found out that certain people within the movement were molesting children and stealing millions of dollars in the name of God. I was completely sickened by that.

One thing I never tolerate as a result of what was done to me as a kid is people who harm children.

Eventually my band broke up in 1988, and once again I struggled with homelessness, crack addiction and a life of crime. This time, I took to robbing drug dealers and had a contract out on my head. I couldn't believe the place I found myself in. How did I get there? I was doing so well.

I had so much promise.

See, I never understood that my life, my healing, would never be complete unless I got out the deep, dark secret of my abuse as a child. In 2000, I began writing a screenplay based on my childhood. I used a lot of the stories, some were even funny, but I would never dare bring to the surface all the things that happened in that home. Actually to this day my two brothers and I have never talked about that.

One night I had a nightmare about it and woke up crying uncontrollably. My girlfriend at the time asked what was wrong, and I told her about EVERYTHING. It was like a huge weight was being lifted off of me as we talked. It all poured out—all the stories—and it was so healing.

Writing for me was therapeutic.

Eventually I wrote my memoir in 2008 entitled, "The Evolution of a CroMagnon," which was praised by literary and film people alike. I'm now adapting it for the big screen and have also written several other scripts. In 2000, I opened a yoga center that teaches yoga for free to people who don't have the money to sit in fancy classes but would like the benefits of what yoga has to offer. It's maintained completely by donations and was open for ten years. I also help run a vegetarian food distribution program for the homeless and have distribution weekly, feeding hundreds at Tompkins Square Park on Manhattan's Lower East Side. Having been homeless and gone hungry myself, many a cold night on the streets, a little hot food in your stomach can make a world of difference.

One of the things I'm very passionate about these days is speaking to kids. I've gone back to Spofford, Lincoln Hall, St. John's Home for Boys and other juvenile centers and lockups, even spoke to gangs in high schools. I show them that I was there, right where they're at now, and that they too can make it if they try. Just never give up. We may have the deck stacked against us, but if we try and never give up we can make it through anything life throws our way. My belief is these kids don't want to hear from people with Ph.D.'s, they want to listen to people that have been there and are going through what they are going through.

In 2013, my second book on plant-based health which takes a funny look at men's diets called, "Meat is for Pussies," was published by Harper Collins. And now my third book is about to be published. I've done TV, been featured on ESPN, radio, in books, newspapers, magazines, done podcasts, countless interviews as well as the talk circuit and people always ask if I could change my upbringing, would I do it? The answer is a definitive NO. See, I thank God every day for how I grew up. My writing teacher Robert McKee says adversity builds character, that pressure is the only revelation of true character. Had I not led such a crazy childhood I wouldn't have become the person I am now and wouldn't have the ability to help the next generation.

I believe as the book *The Four Agreements* states, to "Not Take Things Personal," and that may have been the most difficult thing to do, but it's made me a stronger person.

♡♡♡

John Joseph formed and is the lead singer for the Cro-Mags—an American hardcore punk turned crossover thrash band from New York City - and has been touring the world since 1981.

He penned his memoir in 2007, "The Evolution of a Cro-Magnon" as a way to exercise the demons that haunted him. The response has been overwhelming as John's long-time friend the late Adam Yauch (MCA - Beastie Boys) himself has said, "A lot of people talk about coming from the streets, when John says it, the shit is real."

John's memoir is in development for a feature film, and he has authored his second book, "Meat is For Pussies" (a comedic guide to real health for men). John convinced thousands of people to give up meat and live healthier spiritual lives, and he put his 33 years of experience in the vegetarian/athletic field in every chapter.

He practices the Hare Krishna tenets daily, chanting and doing service for others, feeding the homeless and mentoring at-risk youth. He has competed in six Ironman Triathlons for the charity with several more to complete, including the Kona World Championships.

It seems for John Joseph, life truly has been an evolution.

Thank God I Was Diagnosed with Diabetes

BY JOHN KREMER

I am a night person. I love working at night when the world settles down, all is quiet, and there are no interruptions. That strategy worked well for me for many years as a writer, but eventually it caught up with me.

To keep going late at night—when the earth is so still and silent—I'd snack on junk food, often eating an entire box of cookies or bag of candy. As a result, I gained some 50 pounds over a 20-year period. It was so gradual a change—just a few pounds a year—that it didn't seem so bad. Of course, it was.

I bore the brunt of the weight: walking was harder, muscles ached, getting out of bed got harder and harder. But I loved working at night so much and I couldn't stop the snacking. Truth be told, I was addicted.

I tried diets and would lose a few pounds here and there, but I always gave up on any program within a week or two. Dieting simply wasn't for me. Too many rules.

Then, one May, a number of things began going wrong with my body. The key was my eyesight. I began having trouble reading the words on the computer screen as I wrote. It started with me having to wear my glasses on the tip of my nose so I could read the words clearly.

That worked for a while, but within a week or two, I couldn't push my glasses any further down my nose in order to read.

I discovered another solution for a time. Silly as it seems, I found that I could read the screen if I wore my glasses upside down. That odd strategy worked for another few weeks, but then even that stopped working.

I feared it was old age, that I was losing my ability to see, that my eyes were deteriorating right in front of me. I went to the optometrist and got a new prescription. Again, I could see, but three weeks later, the same problem crept into my routine. I knew I was going to have to see the optometrist again. That was scary. My eyesight was literally degrading minute by minute, hour by hour.

Before I could see the optometrist again, other parts of my body began breaking down. Over the same period of time, I had been getting major calluses on my feet. I thought it was from walking around barefoot so much, which I did when it was hot—and it had been a very hot May and June. One particular dried and cracked callus didn't seem to want to heal at all, no matter how much lotion I slathered on it. This also worried me, but again, I was too busy to do much more than put lotion on my feet several times a day.

I placed the blame on getting older. I was then fifty-five and just figured that it was the cost of aging—a little sooner than I expected. Not having grown old before, I really didn't have a yardstick to go by, except to see other friends also complaining about growing aches and pains.

Then, in late June, I started having another symptom. I had to urinate all the time. Now, on one hand, this was good because it enabled me to drink more water—something my wife had been encouraging me to do. But after a week of urinating on the hour or sometimes more often, I grew concerned that there might be something more going on. So I made an appointment with the doctor (it really takes me getting knocked over the head to visit a doctor). Long story short, he told me I had diabetes.

All the symptoms were there: the rapidly changing eyesight, the cracked and dried skin on my feet, the excessive urination, and other signs I'd ignored. I just didn't know. No one had ever told me.

Diabetes, as it turns out, is not just an inconvenient set of symptoms. It is a life-threatening disease—one that can kill you quickly if ignored.

My doctor described to me my options: drugs, diet change, more exercise, and eventually insulin. None of these options sounded inviting to me. But I did not want to die, so I started making changes.

I didn't want to start taking drugs because, once you do, you really have to keep taking them for the rest of your life. Since I've never been good at taking any sort of pills, whether vitamins, other supplements, or prescription drugs, I knew that really wasn't a viable option for me.

So, slowly, I changed my diet. I ate more vegetables. I cut down on snacks, way down. I drank more water. That wasn't enough. Finally, I discovered Weight Watchers®. I've never been able to stick with other diets because they always felt so restrictive. Don't eat this. Don't eat that. Don't eat at night. Don't do this. Don't do that. Too many "do nots"!

With Weight Watchers®, though, I only count points. As long as I stay within my points, I can eat anything I want, whenever I want. That works for me. Ultimately, we all have to find those little somethings that work for us.

Now my blood sugar is under control. My skin is back to being baby soft. I can see my computer screen without strain. I can read road signs again at night. Most important, I now feel good, even invigorated, as I walk up and down the arroyos near my home in New Mexico. They are steep, but I'm a kid again. My body still complains some, but I am able to move again, get out of bed without that old morning stiffness, and—joy of joys—keep up with my dogs as we walk and sometimes run the arroyos.

I thought I was getting old. I thought I was slowly dying. I thought I had little hope but to go out with a whimper and a sigh.

Thank God I got diabetes. It changed my life. My energy is back. My depression is less. And I've lost 25 pounds, so I'm halfway there to losing those 50 pounds I had gained over so many years.

I still work at night. I can't seem to get away from the deep silence I love so much. But I don't snack anymore. I can't. I want to live.

And, thanks to my diabetes, I am.

♡♡♡

John Kremer *is an acknowledged expert on book publishing and marketing. Besides being the owner of his own publishing company (Open Horizons in Taos, New Mexico), he is also the author of a number of books on publishing and marketing, including 1001 Ways to Market Your Books: For Authors and Publishers (6th Edition), The Complete Direct Marketing Sourcebook, High Impact Marketing on a Low Impact Budget, and Celebrate Today. He is the webmaster of BookMarket.com, QuotableBooks.com, and TouristTrains.us.*

Thank God I Was Raped

BY JULIAN J. GRAYCE

*S*everal years back, if someone told me I would be making such a statement as *"Thank God I was raped,"* I would have considered them cruel and crazy. So, I'm aware of how disturbing this may be for some people to hear or understand. I didn't wake up one day and DING!—suddenly find myself thinking, *"Hey, God ... thanks for the rape."* It was sooo not like that, my friends. It was quite the opposite. I could not understand why God would let this happen to me. I went through unspeakable pain and anguish, and I saw my family's hearts break for me. Yet here I am writing about my rape, and I really am earnestly thankful to God for it! How did that happen? I'll tell you a bit about myself before the rape in hope that you'll see how life so cleverly prepares us for our personal tragedies. It took me some hard, painful years to figure this out. So here is a brief history of my background:

For the first thirteen years of my life, I suffered from a chronic illness. Going through the hardship made me want to help those who were in need. I worked as a crisis counselor, advocate, and support group facilitator for survivors of violent crimes. For ten years I worked directly with victims of sexual assault, rape, incest, elder and child abuse. Working with such heavy situations is draining, and I felt the signs of burnout. Taking a leap of faith, I resigned from my job, and cofounded a consulting business in New York City, where I'd always lived.

But after several years, I felt I owed it to myself to get out of my comfort zone and go to live on the other side of the country.

The several times I'd visited San Francisco, I enjoyed the aesthetics and the laidback attitude of the people there. My family and friends were apprehensive about my moving to a place where I had no friends or established means of income. I understood their concerns, but I was determined to make a life for myself in California, and I went ahead with the relocation.

This was during the dotcom explosion, and most people were willing to pay a disturbing amount of money in cash to get an apartment, something I obviously was not able to do. So after I had found a full-time consultant job, I still needed a part-time job to make ends meet.

I applied for evening and weekend bartending jobs and got a Sunday interview appointment at a high-end restaurant. It was not far from my place. This made me happy because commuting would be easy and the tips would be good. Being new to the city and wanting to take precautions (I am a New Yorker, after all), I asked a new friend to go with me and wait while I interviewed. My counseling experience made me think about safety issues.

The restaurant was both lovely and busy, and the hostess directed me to the manager. After I had given him my resume, he told me to sit at one of the tables while he tended to customers.

Finally he got back to me and proceeded with a friendly and informal interview. I had already learned that in San Francisco, even employers were super casual and laid back. The manager even introduced me to his wife, who was dining with some of their friends. He finally offered me the job and insisted that my companion and I stay and try some of the cuisine so I could become familiar with the food. I thought, How generous! And was happy to get the job.

After some time, the restaurant manager asked me to go to his office to fill out some forms. I told my friend I would be right back. The manager went over to his wife's table and said something to her, then motioned for me to follow him to his office. He was walking quite a bit ahead of me, and I had to take large steps to try to catch up with him. Losing track of where he had gone, I asked an employee, who pointed to the manager's door. When I knocked, he called to me to open the door and come in.

This is when my true journey began. I opened the door but didn't see him. Suddenly, I felt a hand around my face, covering my mouth. He pulled me down to the cold, hard floor. I could not believe it! What was happening? I screamed, but no one heard me. The office was far from the noisy dining room, and no one heard my pleas for help. He held me down and took off my clothes. I struggled, he was too strong ... so strong that the bruise of his handprint on my right arm remained for a couple of weeks. He raped and sodomized me, and I immediately knew that he had done this before because he was so methodical and quite confident that he would not be caught.

Time stood still, and I began to experience what many survivors of trauma describe as an out of body experience: as he raped me I felt like I was watching a movie of someone being raped.

But that someone was not an actor ... it was me, and it was real. I am not sure how much time passed, but when he was done with me, he calmly got himself together while I lay there bleeding, shocked, and in disbelief. Slowly and painfully, I got up to put on my clothes. He turned to me, kissed and thanked me, and walked away. Yes, he did! I could not believe it myself, and it happened to me.

I was no longer the person I was before I opened those doors.

The person before would have thought the same thing that some of you are thinking now, which is, *"Why didn't you run after him and try to kick his ass?"* I tried to fight him off during the rape, but at some point, I disconnected. I was in shock and felt broken. Then denial set in...I just could not accept what had happened to me—after all, I did everything I thought I could to do to be safe. I had someone go with me to the place of the interview, and I told her that I was going to the office and would be right back. The place was crowded, and an employee sent me to the manager's office, so this person knew I was in there with the manager. (Much later, I found out he was his lookout.)

Why didn't the red flags come up? How could I let this happen?

The whole thing was like a nightmare. I don't remember going back into the restaurant's dining room. I finally found my friend, who was waiting for me. She was upset and began to yell at me because I'd taken so long that she thought I'd just forgotten about her. Then suddenly I blurted out, *"I was raped."* Naturally she freaked out. She was very upset. We left the restaurant, and she wanted to call the police. But I said no, and we got a cab home.

Once home, we talked about it, and I decided to call the police. I knew that in rape cases the victim is basically the evidence, so I didn't shower or change my clothes, although every cell in my body wanted to scrub the rapist off me. I could smell him on me, and it made me want to throw up and peel off my skin. The police came, took my report, and drove me to the hospital. They were insensitive and dismissive. I spent about seven hours waiting for a rape crisis nurse to do my rape kit. In the interim, the investigators interviewed me several times. I was in pain and exhausted. When the nurse finally checked me, she said that in all her time doing this type of work, mine was the most terrible physical trauma she'd encountered, adding that she would be more than willing to testify to that in court. She was very kind and compassionate.

I took emergency contraception, an HIV cocktail as a precaution against possible exposure, and an STD test. For weeks, I was weak from the side effects of the HIV cocktail. I was relieved and grateful that my test results were all fine, but can you imagine how awful I felt during those weeks, not knowing if I was okay?! I tried to get counseling, but the referrals I got were not helpful, and I couldn't afford to pay for therapy on my own. I told no one but my sister; I simply worked like a robot, just existing. I didn't know what to do. I didn't eat and couldn't sleep. I just worked. About a month after my rape, I ended up in the emergency room with a severe asthma attack, during which I was pronounced clinically dead for about four minutes. Actually, that was the only time I had felt any peace since the rape. Then I was brought back to my so-called life, and I was not happy to be back!

Why? Why would God be so cruel as to have me go through the agony of physically dying? Why did he tease? I felt the deliciousness of being on the other side. I had peace, absolute love, and joy when I was dead, and then bam! I got the Cosmic BootTM (which I wrote about in detail in my soon-to-be-published book, *Death Didn't Want Me Getting the Cosmic Boot*).

I returned home to finish my recovery and wanted to know about my case, but the investigator was dismissive and unresponsive. I tried many times to find out what was going on, but couldn't get any answers. It took me many months, with the assistance of an advocate, to find out the status of my case: It was closed. The investigator in charge said that I never showed interest in pursuing the case—a completely false statement on his part.

It took years for me to finally have the satisfaction of knowing that my rapist was behind bars for the crime that he committed against me. Even though I was relieved when they put him away where he cannot hurt anyone else, I remained inundated with a rage that was destroying me. After a while of searching, I found a therapist in California who helped a bit. Meanwhile I was trying to live my life, which I did very poorly. I was a walking, talking, breathing ghost, and no matter what I did to help myself, nothing worked. I remained stuck in *"Why did this happen to me?"* and unable to make progress in my healing process.

I went through all the stages common to someone who's had a traumatic incident: denial, shame, self-blame, anger, and so on.

Clinically I knew why I felt and behaved in those ways. But that didn't help me from feeling it. I had worked with rape survivors for many years, and I had taken a self-defense class. I felt that somehow I should have known better, that I should have been able to stop it. I should be able to "get over it" because I knew what steps to take to heal. My life was a complete mess, and I felt no zest for life. I had no direction with work and no personal social life.

After several years in San Francisco, I moved back to New York City and my family found out about the rape— I was no longer functional. I stayed home, unable to go out by myself. I wore baggy clothes and hats, so that no one could see me—even if it were hot outside, I would cover my body. Back in therapy, I still had to take antidepressants and anti-anxiety medication in order to become functional again. The medication helped, but rage still filled me. I simply felt hopeless. I finally decided to end all the pain, so I overdosed on the pills. I ended up in the emergency room, where they gave me an enormous amount of charcoal to help rid my body of the toxins from the pills. I have to tell you there's nothing more mind clearing than seeing the image of yourself with your mouth and teeth stained with thick black coal goop. The thing about hitting rock bottom is that you have only the top to go to. It took me some time to ask myself why I was still in such pain and despair. I knew I was stuck, but how do I give myself the nudge to begin healing?

I thought about when I worked with my clients, and what they shared with me. I remembered the feedback that they gave about me—how compassionate and non-judgmental I was with them. I seriously began to meditate on why I was able to show compassion for others but not for myself. On one of my many sleepless nights, I opened a big box of my old journals and started to read both the pre and post-rape ones, and I sobbed uncontrollably. I finally allowed myself to grieve for the person I had been before the rape. I decided to bury most of my journals symbolically, which allowed me to say goodbye to that part of me that I felt was gone.

But after a while, I realized that part of me was not gone. What the rapist had done had changed me forever. That was a fact! But now it was up to me to decide how it had changed me. Was I going to be a lost soul? Someone scared of her own shadow? Someone who did not trust her judgments anymore? Was I going to continue to see only the ugliness of life and marinate in bitterness?

I re-read the journals from after the rape and tried to objectively see the things that I was going through. I really tried not to judge anything. I just recognized all the things that I had been doing that were not allowing me to heal. I finally did for myself what I was able to do for the clients I worked with: I showed compassion and worked on not being judgmental. By doing so, I ended up forgiving myself. Through doing these things, I became less angry and started the process of letting go of the rage I felt toward my rapist. He overpowered me that night. But I realized that I could have that power back by not letting what he did prevent me from having a happy, fulfilling life. So I simply began to forgive him. This does not mean I wanted to hang out with him and send him holiday cards. But holding on to the rage was not hurting him—it was hurting me. I know it sounds cheesy, but just because it's cheesy doesn't mean it's not true.

I wondered if my working with victims of violent crimes years ago had been a way for God to help me prepare for my own personal tragedy. I know it might sound strange, but I do believe this to be true. Once I took those huge steps of self-compassion, forgiveness, letting go, and reclaiming my life, I reached out to others more and talked openly about my rape. In time, I could again go out by myself and I started literally taking off the layers that I carried. An artist friend of mine knew about my rape and told me about a radio show called The Rape Declaration Forum in New York on radio station WBAI, which his girlfriend hosted and produced. He suggested that perhaps I would want to go on and talk about what had happened to me.

It's a live call-in show, where people can share their story on the air. I decided to do it, and Rebecca Myles, the show's host, invited me to be in the studio while she played my pre-recorded interview.

I went to the studio; it was my first time doing any radio, and I was nervous. After Rebecca played the tape of my story, people called in to share their own stories, saying that in my telling my story I had inspired and helped them. It truly was powerful.

That's when I really began to thank God that I had been raped!

The pain and anger that I had for myself, my rapist, and God had transformed to inner peace and purpose. I was able to see the person I am now—a woman who has survived a personal tragedy and has found her power. I have the power to claim my life. It is me and not my rape that defines it.

I know that compassion and forgiveness starts with me. I know that being in a state of gratitude allows me more things to be thankful for in my life. I have the courage now to be true to myself. I now embrace the writer and artist in me by way of my poems and books. I am an activist and public speaker, spreading the message of self-empowerment and inspiration.

The biggest blessing for me is that I found my purpose: to do radio broadcasting. I was graciously asked to co-host The Rape Declaration Forum at WBAI with Rebecca Myles. I also produce and host my own radio show, The Jay Grayce Radio Variety Show, on Tribecaradio.net.

It is a place of gratitude that allows me to see and understand the great opportunities that can come from my struggles. It has taken me a long time to understand that. I really did not believe that I would find joy in my life again. So for anyone who is lost in despair, I would suggest that you feel what you are feeling. But please also be patient and compassionate with yourself. And I thank God for allowing me the honor of having you read my story.

♡♡♡

Julian J Grayce was a crisis counselor, advocate, and group facilitator for crime victims for ten years before she decided to go in a different career direction, in which she has been an entrepreneur and artist. She is now the creator/producer and host of The Jay Grayce Variety ShowTM for Tribecaradio.net. Julian also is the co-host of The Rape Declaration Forum on New York's WBAI,

99.5 FM. She serves on the board of directors for NPOs and is an activist for victims and animal rights.

Thank God I Died

BY JULIE ANN COHN

I've often heard the expression, *"The third time is the charm."*

Little did I know that it would apply to dying or, as I am often reminded, nearly dying.

Of course, I would not still be "renting" this body if it died completely. I have lived through three near-death experiences. The first two were preparing me for the third—the one that would forever change the course of my life. I've known fear, pain, depression, loss, and denial. I've come to know gratitude, joy, health, love, harmony, and abundance. I've been blessed with success to counter hardship.

Death is not a hardship, but, at times, "living" having known the "peace of death" is a hardship.

The first time I crossed to the "other side"—the place where time ends, spirit resides, and I left this body of mine—was when I was 19.

Like many at my age, I had taken a break from college to experiment with the hippie culture. I met a man named Osiris. He had long hair, golden skin, and a beautiful smile. It felt as though I had stepped out of the book called, My Life, and into a fantasy of love, music, and drugs.

At first, we lived in a penthouse apartment in West Los Angeles.

Life seemed grand. He worked for a school supplies business, and I was a salesperson at Judy's.

Then we moved to the Valley in Southern California—and lived in a trailer. Along with friends, we ran a health food restaurant. It was there that he got addicted to nitrous oxide—also known as laughing gas. We had tanks of it in the back for baking.

One time Osiris brought one of the tanks home to the trailer. He started sucking on the gas. At first, this just relaxed him and put him to sleep.

Then one night—out of the blue—as he was doing his usual gas, the tube started whipping around out of his mouth. I reached over to turn it off and—BAM!

Osiris grabbed a knife, cut me twice, threw me out of the trailer, and left me for dead on the ground, bleeding.

I have no idea how I managed to get myself into my car, drive back over the hill to my parent's house, and then fall on the horn in their driveway. My white silk shirt was drenched in blood.

I was watching myself from above.

I remember seeing my father move me into his car, saying, *"I hope this taught you a lesson,"* and drive me to a hospital.

From that point on I was gone.

I did not have an awareness of light, or any of the things I experienced later the third time I visited "beyond." In fact, it seemed to me that I was just floating . . . until the "knowing" came. I woke up in the hospital knowing I had been through something very powerful. Contrary to how it was all perceived, I felt like I had received something wonderful. Of course, no one understood, and many tried to point out the awfulness of the situation.

But I knew I had walked in the Light—if only for moments (hours actually) ... life was amazing.

After recovering, I went back into "my life" at college—a bit wiser, and a whole lot more curious about metaphysical, spiritual things.

The second time I journeyed "beyond" was when I was 35.

I had been working in advertising moving up the ladder. One of the perks I used to get was Kings Hockey tickets. I mean—great seats. It was the third period of the Stanley Cup Playoffs. The game was tied.

I went to the bathroom during a break. While there, a woman sprayed hairspray all over the place.

As I returned to my seat, I began losing my air.

Although I didn't know it at the time, I was having a severe asthma attack. I was wheezing, coughing, and screaming for the Kings. The man sitting next to my now ex-husband—then husband—kept nudging him, saying, *"Maybe you should get her out of here."*

When I heard this, I proclaimed, *"No f***g way! This is a playoff game."*

By the time we got to the car—I was not breathing.

White light was surrounding me.

There was an unsettling inner peace that came over me—unsettling because I felt afraid. I felt stuck. Then I fought to come back. I wanted to live. I wanted to breathe. I wanted to continue.

We went to the hospital, and I know from what they tell me that they had to put a shot of adrenaline in my heart to get it started again. I was pumped full of steroids to open my breathing passages.

Again, I experienced a sense of floating.

My "return" this time was different.

It felt like an abrupt interruption—for all of a sudden, I felt my body again, heart pumping fast, grasping for air. I knew I had just experienced something extraordinary. I was aware of every breath I took. The gift of life was in my breath. I awoke with a great appreciation for air, for color, and for those who loved and supported me.

I understood that life is precious. I was so grateful to be alive.

Now fade to black.

I am 39.

It is a beautiful day.

I am at the top of my game in advertising, loving life, and having fun. I had become a typical Type A personality—an achiever. My employees referred to me as their "Hippie Boss" for my unconventional management style. I loved what I did.

It is three days before the third time I died. I had four of my most trusted staffers in my office speaking about the company's insurance policy, and I said, *"Someday, I want to do what I love, without having to think about money."* I knew that my career was not who I am, and I wanted to do something that reflected more of who I am, even though it may not be as financially rewarding.

We all mused at this notion, and all expressed a sigh of, *"Oh well,"* at the passing thought.

Three days later, I decided to leave work a bit early at 4:30 pm. It was September 18, 1998. I was driving my hot black '96 Corvette south on 405, going about 30 miles an hour in traffic.

All of a sudden—WHAM!

My car spun out of control into oncoming traffic.

Then again—WHAM!—as the same black car hit my car, spinning me in the opposite direction.

I thought, *"Oh my God, that guy just hit me!"* I tried desperately to control my car. But my brakes, airbag, and seatbelt all failed. I felt my fingers rip off my hand...

My car landed head-on in the center divider. My blood was everywhere.

My spine was severed, and my lower back was broken. My fingers lay on the freeway. My arm was broken, my leg destroyed, and the seatbelt ripped across my stomach.

I screamed my last words, *"I have insurance!"*

A doctor stopped on the opposite side of the freeway and picked up my fingers, taping them to my hand. Five women in a white SUV stopped to call 911. There was so much blood...and I was gone.

I remember being surrounded by that familiar white light.

My younger brother—who died of AIDS at 30—was there, healed and whole. My grandparents were there— and my cat...

All of them perfect, welcoming.

I remember beautiful, vibrant colors.

It was warm, safe and beautiful.

I was shown pictures of my life. Still shots. And only one question was asked with each picture I saw: What does this have to do with love?

I was not aware of the horror I had just been through. I was only aware of that single question, What does this have to do with love? It is not as if I were answering, rather just knowing that love is what my life was and is about.

I had no concept of time.

I remember feeling like I didn't want to leave this place.

Then the voice came to me. It told me in no uncertain terms that I had to go back and heal the world—in exchange, I would walk with angels—and be able to return whenever I wanted.

The next thing I know—I'm back in my broken, bruised, pain-riddled body.

All I know is horrific pain. Then the drugs. Morphine, Methadone, and so many others—all designed to distance me from the pain, depression, fear, anxiety, and despair of my circumstances.

I thought my life was shattered; that my dreams were gone.

I was at my lowest low ever.

Doctors told me the worst: *"You will never walk again ... you will never be out of pain ... you may not have the same use of your hands."*

And then there were surgeries. Some 20 procedures to correct the nerve root damage in my spine. Only to be followed by the news, *"The damage is non-repairable. This is as good as it gets."*

Wow.

To look at me today—except for a few scars—you may not know what I lived through. You may not know that I do have pain in my body 24/7—even though I don't use drugs. You would not know that it took two years of working with a team of doctors, physical therapists, and alternative medical modalities to get me where I am today. You would not know that I struggled in denial trying to recreate my old life, only to find that I was not the same. You would not know that I sunk so far into pain that I tried to die again—just to get back to that place of inner peace, tranquility, and love. You would not know that I went through major drug withdrawals.

To look at me today, you would not know the anger I harbored for years before appreciating the hit-and-run driver who left the scene... Caltrans for not capturing the accident on the cameras poised over that section of the 405... the lawyers who advised me not to sue GM—because I would run out of money before they would—giving them the opportunity to counter-sue for malicious prosecution ... the doctors who could not cure me, and who only "practiced" medicine ... and of course me for having left work early that day and getting into the accident in the first place.

To look at me today, you would not know that I choose life every single day. To look at me today, you would not know I studied, reinvented myself, and found my way back to loving life. To look at me today, you would not know I am a miracle of love, light, faith, and perseverance.

Today you would look at me and wonder, *"Where does she get that amazing energy? She is so filled with love and light ... her smile is so bright."*

Today I live in and reflect gratitude. I am not just thankful for my life, but for everything I have been through. Yes, I am doing what I love—without thinking about money. I am a living example of "Be careful what you wish for"—stay conscious all the time. I am so grateful I know that life/love/spirit and my work move through me and are not of me. I became a master transformational healer, a teacher, a life coach, and an author. I am still a marketing wizard doing consulting even today.

I'm blessed.

I know God and spirit, and walk with and see angels.

I know the magic of life, the wonder of each blue sky.

I am not who I used to be—I am better.

Thank God I died—for it gave me life.

♡♡♡

Julie Ann Cohn—graduated from UCLA with BA's in English and Theatre, and from The Royal Academy of Dramatic Arts, London, with a Master's in Theatre and holds a Doctorate in Metaphysics. Julie is world-renowned in her healing & teaching work, having taught and provided healing to clients in Israel, London, Brazil, Bulgaria & Australia. She is also founder and co-creator of The Blend™ & an active partner in Silver Unicorn Spirit Gifts. A partial list of her spiritual credentials include: Usui Reiki Master, Magan David Life Energy Master, Vibrational Healer, Sufi Reiki Master, Shaman, Crystal Resonance Therapist & Ordained Minister.

In addition to her current work as a Performance Coach, Reiki Master/Healer, Database Marketing Guru and #1 Best-selling author, Julie was CEO of J-Team Database Marketing, Inc., Founder of a newly created power organization Zoomer`A La Carte. She is also a certified Coach giving service to incarcerated individuals through the "Getting Out By Going In" (GOGI) Program. "Work," she says, "feeds my soul!" Julie wrote a 46-Week Personal Empowerment Program for inmates.

She brings 30+ years as a highly accomplished Database Marketing Guru advertising executive with a stellar reputation. Julie sits on many corporate boards of directors and advisory boards. She is an honored lifetime member of The Continental Who's Who, and a mentor for The National Association of Professional Women.

Julie is a three-time NDE Survivor, Living Miracle, Tempo and Echo Award winner, #1 best-selling co-author in How Did You Do That?, co-author in #1 best-selling series "Thank God I, Volume 2", "111 One Pages of Wisdom", and author of the book "CASH—Creating Achievement & Success Harmoniously", the book "Introduction to Crystals", and more.

Thank God I Died and Lost Half My Brain

BY KAREN ORELL

*T*he incredible beauty of the sunny fall day didn't portend a hint that everything in my life was about to take a huge turn down a new path. I was just starting across a five-lane, one-way road when I saw a car swerving into my lane.

He was coming toward me on the two-lane road I was driving on. His car on the opposite side of the intersection from mine.

"And this joker thinks he can turn left before I get through the intersection!" I exclaimed to myself.

I'd just left an important organizing project with stacks of papers now covering counters, tables, and floors, to give myself a two-and-a-half-hour break. Just enough time to enjoy the special facial my sister had gifted me and I didn't want to be late.

My phone GPS called out directions, bringing my thoughts back into the car. I looked again to see, yes indeed the joker was now squarely in my lane driving

125

towards me head on. My utter disbelief shifted to my mind racing for any way to avoid hitting him. I slammed on the brake with my right foot and braced my left foot hard against the floor of the car pushing my back into the seat. My arms locked solidly on the steering wheel pressing my head hard against the headrest behind me. But no matter how hard I pressed the brakes my car continued skidding forward.

Then everything went into slow motion, each and every moment expanding to be an eternity. I was sure these were the last moments I would be on Earth. My incredible life flashed before me; world travel, owning multiple businesses and my two children. I felt at peace. Yes, I was ready to go if this was my time…

I heard the silver Saturn screeching towards me, headed dead-on for the front of my car.

"God, I'm ready to leave if this is my time," I said out loud.

A split second after saying that, everything disappeared. There was only complete blackness. No sound, no light, no color, no feeling. I was a point of consciousness in a great expansiveness of complete blackness. Like being suspended inside a black hole somewhere out in the middle of the universe far, far away.

"This must be the passageway to Heaven," I thought to myself. I kept searching for the light I'd heard so much about for years in my spiritual studies. But there was nothing but eternal darkness. I decided maybe I was in purgatory, a way station before passing over.

Then there was a voice, softly at first and far away. As I turned my attention to the voice, it got louder and started drawing me towards it. Suddenly, I was back in my body in the front seat of my car. At least what was left of it. A man was shaking me and yelling, *"Get out of the car!"*

There was smoke everywhere and my throat and lungs burned from the chemicals in the air. I tried to move my arms and legs, but nothing happened. He continued talking to me as he leaned across to unbuckle my seatbelt. I looked up, the glowing sunlight creating a beautiful halo behind his head, outlining his long dark curly hair. He looked like Jesus.

"You've got to get out of the car," I heard the voice repeating. I sat frozen unable to move. I felt myself slipping away again, my eyes only staying open another second.

When I opened them again, I found myself on the sidewalk looking at pieces of the two cars all over the road, smoke and fluids pouring out from the front of mine.

"Where's the man who got me out of the car?" I started asking people in the crowd that had formed.

"What man?" they asked looking at me blankly.

I was shaking uncontrollably, trying to piece everything together. Dizzy, in a fog of confusion, my throat and chest burning from the toxic chemicals the airbag released. Every breath was like having acid poured down my throat. As I sat there in a zombie-like trance, the fact that I hadn't died was sinking in. Since I really thought I was going to die, I was struggling with why I was sitting there staring at a giant heap of wreckage.

"I must still have a lot of work left to do," I said firmly to myself almost as a pledge.

Unbeknownst to me at that moment, my darkest fear had come true. Losing my mental capacity. As the first days of being in shock started to shift into being in excruciating constant pain, I started to realize numerous things I was no longer able to do. My thinking processes became a jumbled mess of electrical signals pinging around in my aching head, unable to put together any semblance of meaningful thought.

Two days after the accident I got up after another sleepless night of writhing in pain. I started for the bathroom, took three steps and stopped. What was I going to do? I stood in the middle of my bedroom to get any inkling of whatever it was I had planned to do when my mind went completely blank. I knew the brain's job was to answer any question you ask it, why wasn't mine!

"What was I going to do? What was I going to do? What was I going to do?" I repeated out loud. Nothing came to my mind. No matter how hard I tried to concentrate, nothing crystallized as an answer. As I tried to think my head got very hot like it was going to burn up and it hurt even more. I tried to hold my head in my hands to sooth it but my touch created searing pain across my forehead. Since I couldn't move my neck, I turned my body slowly to look around the room for some clue of my intentions. The stabbing pain on the sides of my head was the feeling of someone pounding an ice pick into my skull. I froze hoping it would stop if I held still. More pain shooting up

my spine, then a shock-like pain pierced my low back and I fell to the floor.

While I lay there I searched for any solution, even a partial to reduce my pain.

Eating may make me feel better, I thought. If it doesn't help with the pain, at least I can take some painkillers the doctor gave me since taking them on an empty stomach made me vomit.

I laboriously moved down the staircase to my kitchen holding the walls on either side, terrified I would fall down the stairs. I couldn't actually feel the steps with my numb feet and leaned slightly forward to watch that I stopped on each one.

I stood in the middle of the kitchen blankly staring into my pantry. Finally putting a pan on the stove, I turned it on high, and slowly picked up a box of quinoa scrutinizing the instructions. The sentences were out of order and didn't make sense. I blinked and looked again, concentrating harder, but the letters didn't come into focus and stabbing pain shot through my eye sockets. What little I had seen of the words were jumbled up and made no sense.

Since even standing was incredibly difficult, there was only one option. I lay on my side motionless on the living room floor filled with deep confusion, sadness, and loss. Streams of tears running down my face into the carpet as I grieved for all the things I could no longer do. The pain was so overpowering I held as still as possible and prayed it would pass.

As I continued to mourn the loss of who I was just days ago, I smelled something burning. It was coming from the kitchen. I didn't want to move but knew I had to find out what it was. There was a fiery red pan on the stove and smoke filling the kitchen. I couldn't remember putting it there, but since I was the only person in the house, I must have.

This was unbelievable! *"I'm now not even safe to stay in the house by myself,"* I thought in disgust. Not only was I not getting better, I was getting worse with each passing day. I didn't recognize myself. I wished I had died in the accident.

"I give up," I said out loud, deciding that surrender was the only path available. For me to have said this was a major life change. I don't give up. I tough it out through almost anything, but this was different. I had no choice.

This was my daily life for months and months, struggling to accomplish even basic tasks. To survive, I had to move from needing to control everything into a place of total surrender. The airbag injury to my head and neck caused injuries that left me unable to read or write. My senses of hearing, taste, vision and touch were all damaged to the point of feeling disconnected from my body and the world around me. Along with these physical and mental challenges, I was suffering with a severe and deep depression that was unlike anything I'd ever experienced. Earlier in my life I was able to work my way out of depression with supplements, diet, and physical activities like dancing. This was not the case now, nothing seemed to help or improve my mental state. I came to a huge realization of how having a brain injury affects moods and not something you can "work your way out of." This gave me incredible empathy and understanding of what those with severe mental illness and depression go through.

Over the next two years I saw over 15 medical professionals and spent hundreds and hundreds of hours in analysis, medical tests, physical therapy, doctor appointments and getting injections. All this in between legal appointments for the lawsuit for reimbursements. My car loss and medical costs were over $100,000 now. Months passed, and I saw only slight improvements in my physical and mental state.

Through the long period of being unable to care for myself, I realized that my life of "go it alone" and always doing everything myself would have to change. I began to reach out to others, especially close family and friends for help. Asking for help was difficult for me, but I found how happy others were to do things for me. I realized that by doing everything myself, I'd stolen some of their joy in giving.

A major challenge was the invisible nature of my injuries. I couldn't look at my brain and see what was injured. Some clues I had were a non-existent memory and complicated thought processes completely escaping me. The confusion about the damage finally cleared up when I found a brain research group to explain it. Nearly 20 electrical leads were attached to my head while I did various tasks, such as reading, with machines recording my brain patterns. Their reports detailed the specific areas of my brain that were damaged and the corresponding functions they controlled. Getting these results gave me the insight to move forward with a full commitment to recovery. I had information, hope and a pathway to healing my brain. I now truly saw *"the light at the end of the tunnel,"* and with inspiration to dedicate myself to my life's work and mission.

With my newly directed intention for restoration, I learned how magnificent and regenerative the body and mind are. Healing can happen and recovery is attainable, even when it doesn't look possible. It took time, commitment to a daily regimen and support from others. But slowly I was able to regain my mental abilities and my body became the resilient structure I'd known all my life.

Looking back now, I realize that this healing process brought me to a rededication to the work I have left to do here on Earth–becoming all I can be and facilitating others to do the same. When I feel overwhelmed, I remember the accident and that I'm here for a reason. Each day I ask, *"Am I doing what's important to my life mission?"* The accident and its memory remain a constant reminder of the thin veil between the two worlds of living and dying.

Now my intention with the actions and activities I engage in has become of utmost importance to me. I still enjoy tackling a menacing pile of paperwork, but not just for the feeling of being in control, it's about something deeper. My accident became the vehicle for me to honor all life and express gratitude in my daily living. I value my time incredibly and see each moment here on earth as a gift to be cherished. My connection to spirit is even stronger, and I am moved to incorporate spirit into all the work I do. I never thought the day would come when I would say, *"Thank God I died and lost half my brain!"*

And every now and then I remember the voice that bade me to leave the car and the vision of a man standing in a halo of light, and I wonder …

♡♡♡

Karen Orell is an internationally-recognized speaker, author, and leader, whose life-changing expertise has touched the lives of thousands through her radio shows, television appearances, travel tours and live events. Combining her 30 years of business and entrepreneurial experience with training in psychology, shamanism and spirituality she inspires, mentors and empowers others to achieve and live their greatest dreams.

Karen mentors those who are ready for positive and purposeful transformation, offering life-changing programs to one-on-one clients, groups and through live events. She calls San Diego California home but travels extensively meeting with clients, leading workshops and special events.

Find out ways to tap into your full potential at www.karenorell.com.

Karen is offering a free gift to the Thank God I audience which you can claim at www.KarenOrell.com/FreeGift.

Thank God I Met the Man Who Mugged Me

BY LORRAINE GARNETT

I was in my usual mind fog.

There was a time when secretly in my head, I'd hum and chant and repeat the same phrases until I'd feel like my brain was in a knot that kept getting tighter and tighter.

Outside my head, in the world of time and matter, I was said to have a listening problem. I was said to have a problem relating. And doctors argued over what could be done for me.

One evening, while I was in this mind fog—I'll call it that since there was disagreement as to the diagnosis—a chance encounter with a stranger showed me a new way of being in the world.

As I found out later, I'd been zigzagging along New York's Park Avenue. I was on my way to a dreaded dinner at my least favorite uncle's when I heard a voice that wasn't mine and didn't come from inside me.

"Keep walking!" it hissed in my ear.

I felt the shock of being rudely awakened from my private reverie.

He was very tall, he towered over me, and as I looked up at him, I uncharacteristically made eye contact. Normally, I'd involuntarily turn my gaze away from people's faces, as if some mysterious force controlled the movement of my head and eyes.

"Why?" I asked, still not comprehending.

"Because," he said, *"There's a razor at your throat."*

For no more than a nano-second, I felt something cold graze my skin. Then he opened his hand just long enough for me to see a metallic flash. I remember marveling at what skill he had—he'd made his point without actually cutting me.

"Don't make me hurt you," he warned. *"I'm gonna take you to where no one can see us. Then I'm gonna rob you. Then I'm gonna set you free. But if you try and holler, or even look at me suspicious, I'll cut up your pretty face so bad, no man'll look at you ever again."*

As he spoke, my habitually knotted brain snapped to attention. Unaccustomed as I was to the real world's sharp edges, I felt strange, not at all like myself.

I put my arm around him, as requested. I was too stunned to feel any fear.

We reached the corner of Park and 36th Street, directly across from my uncle's building. The doorman was looking in our direction. I might make a run for it, I thought... but my captor was too quick for me. Alerted by his ready animal instinct, and sensing the doorman's eye, he tightened his grip, and with an invisible movement, jabbed my collarbone with the side of his razor. Again, I marveled at his skill.

"Talk to me," he demanded in a harsh whisper, *"Make like we're having a conversation."*

Now, the art of conversation had not been one of my strong points. My mind would go blank, my mouth would feel cottony—it was hard enough talking to relatives. What could I say to this stranger?

But I surprised myself.

I heard myself speaking, bantering actually, in an easy, confident voice that I barely recognized as mine.

"This is one of those things that always happens to other people ..." I said.

To which my captor responded, completing my sentence, *"... but never happens to you!"*

"Think of what a great story you'll have ..." he continued. To which I said, *"Someday I'll tell my grandchildren about my big, bad mugger."* And he said, *"You'll have such a great story, you'll want me to mug you all over again!"*

We both broke up laughing. And while we were laughing, I felt that he had loosened his grip.

We turned the corner and headed west in the direction of the garment district. By now we were walking arm in arm, the rhythm of our strides were in sync with one another's.

Suddenly, I remembered—I only had five dollars on me! When I was growing up, a kid on our block was killed by a pissed-off mugger, supposedly for not having enough cash on him. I realized I would have to break the bad news to my captor.

Again, I found myself speaking in a voice that seemed to be coming from somewhere outside myself.

"Your time is worth money. All I have is a cheap watch and five lousy dollars. Not worth your valuable time. The sooner you let me go, the sooner you can move on and find a better prospect."

I was scared, of course, of what he might do to me. But I was also proud of myself. I'd just spoken up, I'd asserted myself, and I thought I sounded really businesslike.

My captor responded by muttering a string of profanities, which were directed at fate in general, and at his own misjudgment for choosing me. Although he still held me at razor point, I started seeing him as just another plodding soul—I actually felt a pang of empathy for him.

He told me that, yes, I wasn't worth his trouble, but he would nonetheless have to take me to where he was taking me.

"It's because I live by my rules," he said. *"Nothing personal, but I got my rules and they save my ass and my biggest rule is no one gets free if there's a police officer they can run into."*

I looked around and pointed out that there were no police officers within my field of vision. But he would have none of it.

"People's attention is like a strainer, full of cracks and holes. Everyone's got their blind spots. And you, pretty lady, you got a blind spot big enough for a whole precinct to hide out in it."

He told me how he'd followed me earlier, how he'd sized me up.

"You had no idea I was behind you—sure, I was wearing sneakers and I'm good at coming up on people—but, still, I could tell you didn't know what was going down—I stay alive because I know what people see and what they don't see."

"What exactly was I doing that made you single me out?"

"The way you were walking, all crooked and dreamlike. Gotta learn to walk in a straight line, walk fast, look purposeful, and here's an inside secret–any time you feel like you're in danger, hold your keys in your hand in front of you."

In the years to come, I would remember the key trick, courtesy of my mugger.

"I don't mess with no one holding keys," he said. *"Keys can cut someone's eye out."*

By now, the street was almost empty–which made me start seriously wondering as to his real intention. *"I see you're a professional at what you do,"* I said, hoping that this might flatter him. But he went silent on me, as if thinking something to himself.

"I meant that as a compliment," I continued, *"You're super smart, you've got amazing skills ..."* but, still, he said nothing.

What I said next–I don't know how I came up with it–was an offhand remark that turned out to be my ultimate being-present-in-the-moment high point:

"What's a nice guy like you doing in a job like this?"

My captor burst out laughing.

He stomped his feet, slapped his thighs, roared, and struggled to catch his breath. Something had shifted in that moment.

"You're the nicest person I mugged all day," he said, still gasping to be able to speak. *"I wish all my muggees were nice like you!"*

I could have made a getaway then, but now there was no need to. My captor—he was no longer that—had let go of me during his laughing fit.

When we arrived at his chosen spot—an empty lot not far from the river—he announced, *"Well, this is it, the place where I conduct my business."*

I reached down into my purse and handed him my wallet. It turned out I didn't have five dollars—four dollars and change, to be exact. As he took the money, we joked that it's too bad he didn't take credit cards.

Next, he removed my watch—at which point he noticed the ring I was wearing. It was an antique cameo that I'd worn since I was little. As he tried to pull it off my finger, he noticed that I was crying.

"Sentimental value?"

"Yes."

"Then keep it," he told me and said I was free to go.

But I didn't go—at least not yet. We'd been walking in lockstep, our bodies close, his arm draped over my shoulder. He thinks I'm pretty, I thought.

I reached up and kissed him.

I turned to walk away a few moments later, then stopped and looked back over my shoulder. *"I wish we'd met under different circumstances,"* I told him— and meant it.

He waved and smiled and left me with these words: *"Don't get caught by no muggers!"*

Later that evening as I was trying to explain why I was late to my uncle—and my uncle accused me of "making up excuses"—I realized that I was somehow different. I didn't sulk, nor did I get angry. Here was one bully who would no longer get the best of me.

In the days and weeks that followed, I took to heart what I'd learned about body language. Until my mugger pointed it out to me, I'd been clueless to what my body was doing. I enrolled in acting classes and in time would study dance and martial arts. I became acutely aware of my body in space, and by extension my presence in the world. I took ownership of my effect on others and how they behaved toward me.

As a "muggee," conventional thinking told me I was a victim. But my experience taught me otherwise. Thanks to my mugger, I first experienced the full force of focused awareness—so I know how powerful I can be.

As I work today at assisting others to write about what's hidden in the cracks in their awareness, I thank the man who mugged me from the bottom of my heart.

♡♡♡

Lorraine Garnett is ThankGodi's chief story-writing coach and advisor. She is a feature screenplay writer, Emmy-nominated TV writer, and advertising copywriter. Lorraine served as Artistic Director of New York's D-Stages Playwrights' Development Lab. Her credits include writing one of the best-known advertising slogans ever.

Thank God I Didn't Give Up

BY MARSH ENGLE

I sat at the edge of the cold examining table. This was a familiar place. And, it wasn't comfortable. Even though I'd been in many rooms just like this one before. A birth condition requiring multiple surgeries with long, drawn out recoveries made hospitals, needles, tests and physicians a familiar environment. But, this time was different, very different.

As I waited for the doctor to walk through the door of his examination room, I was given space to pause to remember the magnitude of what had brought me here to his office. It wasn't easy, those past months of not knowing why my energy was dropping day after day, why it was nearly impossible to climb out of bed each morning. It wasn't easy waiting for test result after test result, poking and prodding for answers to no avail. It wasn't easy being scared—at times terrified—about my future. My heart told me this was not a simple health problem to be overlooked or dismissed. My spirit urged, *"Do not give up looking for the answer. If you do, you will die."*

Answers Begin to Emerge
I don't know if he didn't have the courage to tell me. Or, if it was an uneasy embarrassment from the times he had

142

told me the tests were inconclusive and nothing could be detected. Or, the many times he had determined it as stress, or simply my over-reaction to a minor health concern. Maybe so, after all, it had taken my strong and relentless insistence that an MRI test be completed just to make certain that the blood tests weren't missing something, something that would show us the answer— give a hint to what was stealing my vibrancy, my health and possibly my future.

When the doctor handed me the test results, all he could say is, *"I recommend that you make an appointment with UCLA Medical Center. They may be able to help you."* He said nothing more. He simply left the examination room. UCLA is a teaching hospital recognized for treating unusual cases. I assumed that the doctor had given up on the search for answers, feeling that he had exhausted his resources. Minutes later, I left his office and headed home, report in hand.

As I settled myself in the tiny apartment where my son and I were now living, I opened the envelope and began to read the complicated collection of medical jargon, words that left me puzzled but longing to understand. There was one sentence, however, that stood out very bold and clear.

The sentence read: *"Strong evidence of the presence of lymphoma."* The report went on to give recommended treatment. Shocked, I whispered to myself, *"I think this report says that I have cancer. The doctor who determined this diagnosis—clearly—has no idea who I am."*

Breakdowns Before Breakthroughs

The months leading up to the diagnosis had been tough ones. The shock of my mother's sudden and unexpected death a few months earlier continued to plague me with waves of grief and deep sadness beyond any emotion I'd ever experienced. My once thriving business, the one I had built from the ground floor up while raising my two young sons as a single mother, was now failing. My days were long, stressful, doing all I could to simply keep up.

It's true. I'd denied the early symptoms that, looking back now, I can see had been showing themselves for months. But now the downward spiraling of my health could no longer be denied. Change was needed, desperately— immediately. The diagnosis confirmed it. Scared and alone, I now faced a search for the answer and the fight to save my life.

A Journey of Healing

"The doctors clearly have no idea who I am." Those nine words continued to play through my thoughts—over and over—reminding me of a power to heal, encouraging the search for more answers.

But, where does one begin to heal their life? What changes are needed?

Following the diagnosis, I immersed myself in learning about the disease. I wanted to know it intimately. Meet it face to face. Even make friends with it. Sounds crazy but I believe this may be the very thing that changed everything. I studied. Met with experts. Spoke with more doctors. Read. And, allowed myself to be guided to more answers. Essentially, I surrendered to my deeper Self, the part of me that believed healing possible. I listened to the voice within that continued to remind, *The doctors clearly have no idea who I am.*

The Journey Within

A healing journey can be very isolating. Surrounded by people, I felt more alone than I'd ever felt. Friends didn't know what to say. My sons were silent. The fear-inducing words and opinions of the doctors and all that I read were unsettling and scary.

After weeks of being immersed in looking outside for answers, a dynamic thought suddenly occurred to me, an awareness that would ultimately change the course of my life: *Before I can do anything more, before healing can truly take place, I must go within—I must ignite the spiritual power to heal.*

I declared a 'sacred yes' to do exactly that. And, with that 'sacred yes' became a spiritual practice and commitment to dive deep into study and growing and learning.

Up until now my healing journey was always directed by traditional medicine. Energy medicine was a foreign idea. Now I found myself studying with shamans. Sat for hours in meditation. Absorbed the beauty of nature with long hikes, keeping my body moving. I wrote volumes of words in journals. All the while, traveling deep into my heart.

The Sacred 'Yes'

My 'sacred yes' came to be a power-packed agreement— an agreement that would focus towards the faith and knowing of my deeper Self—an agreement that would not only serve as a replenishing force for my physical body, but also pointed towards the renewing of my mind and of my spirit.

I agreed to grow beyond the defined
To begin, I was clear that things weren't working as they once did. So, I must be willing to let go of the old definitions. To do this meant stepping into the unknown and expanding my relationship with intuitive guidance. It meant exploring non-traditional means of healing and allowing for new ways of co-creating my life.

I agreed to find the yes in all things
Forgiveness became a power ally that changed my life immediately. It allowed for a new, fresh perspective. I dug deep to find where I was holding on to doubt, shame, guilt, and anger—then, I forgave myself. And, I forgave others and asked for their forgiveness. Finally, I forgave the circumstances of my life. Through a moment-by-moment practice of forgiveness, something magical happened. An expansive flow of gratitude began to spring forth. I found myself grateful for EVERYTHING.

I agreed to ignite the power of new possibilities
I found the flow of gratitude to be an inspired motivating power. My practice of gratitude pointed my eyes in the direction of seeing possibilities that I may have at one time overlooked or undervalued. By taking away the blinders of judgment, fear and doubt, I began to see new opportunities, uncover new answers and new solutions— they naturally appeared.

I agreed to collaborate with sheer trust
Trust. Always a challenge, it seemed. But, as I let go and leaned in to trust more and more, something occurred to me. There are really only two choices ever: Worry. Or, trust. And, either choice requires the same: Faith in the unknown. Choose worry and I was putting my trust in fear of the future. Place my attention in the direction of trust and I allowed grace to point the way.

I agreed to play with fresh possibilities
The more I became comfortable in trusting the unknown, the more life presented answers. My mantra became: "Be alert. Life is showing you the way." Synchronicity became an everyday occurrence. Chance meetings with healers, energy workers, physicians and treatment solutions began to show up in the most unexpected and unanticipated ways.

I agreed to bring my radiance to life
This agreement: the most powerful of all. I declared a 'sacred yes' to answer the one true calling of my life: to set free my innate gifts and wisdom that had once been vastly undervalued; to see the purpose of every experience; and, to acknowledge how every event brings with it divine meaning. In the end, I came to recognize, as author Joseph Campbell said best: *"The privilege of a lifetime is being who you are."*

♡♡♡

Though best known as a highly inspired motivational speaker and mentor to entrepreneurial women worldwide, **Marsh Engle** *is also a respected marketing advisor to small business leaders and start-ups. She consults with major corporations and media studios on women's brand initiatives.*

On a mission to create positive shifts in the culture of women's leadership, her groundbreaking programs, special events and speaking engagements have been instrumental in launching the success of thousands worldwide. She is a multi-published author of three books and creates meaningful campaigns to generate worldwide impact. She's been awarded a United States

Congressional Proclamation for the establishment of AMAZING WOMAN'S DAY and is founder of THE ONE MILLION CALLED TO LEAD, a movement dedicated to providing women the resources to create a life of meaning by building successful projects, careers, brands and businesses positioned to benefit millions!

Marsh Engle Radio broadcasts each week on VoiceAmerica Women, where she speaks to a global audience about what it takes to create careers of passion and businesses with impact.

For more information about Marsh Engle and her work, visit: www.MarshEngle.com

Thank God My Baby Was Taken From Me

BY MICHELLE PATTERSON

*T*oday, as I sit here and write, I know I'm about to change my life. I'm scared more than anything at the very thought of the world knowing my secret, but I also want to be finally free.

I remember my ex-boyfriend breaking up with me. He'd met this older girl from another town, and his life had moved on. I felt completely gutted. I lost my appetite. I couldn't concentrate. I lost interest in everything.

Then, within a short time, I found out I was pregnant. I remember the look on my mum's face when she told me, in no uncertain terms, that neither my ex-boyfriend, nor anyone else, was to be told. This began the era in my life of keeping secrets about secrets.

You know that feeling when your heart sits in someone else's hands? My self-worth plummeted, and I felt lower than the lowest scum. The judgment word "slut" lay silently on my lips. My already shaky relationship with my mum declined into detachment, and I felt judged and controlled.

149

I was sent off to Sydney, to live with my Aunty Beryl (my mum's best friend), and where my Great Aunty Dot drove me to my appointments at the hospital.

Living there in secret was like living in a prison.

On one of the rare times I went out, we went to the markets in town, and I spotted a girl and her parents from my home town. Straight away, we all panicked and quickly ran out to the car before anyone could see me.

Then there was Aunty Beryl's daughter who was the same age as me. She'd be on the phone a lot, or going out places with her friends, or spending a lot of time with her boyfriend. It was really hard for me, being as I was a social outcast.

In hindsight, I realize that during this overwhelming time, I began to forge a relationship with Aunty Beryl. She spoke and reasoned with me differently… conversations that were impossible to hold with my mum.

Meanwhile, my mind kept swinging back and forth between wanting to get this baby out of me and then my life could go back to normal, and not wanting to let my child go. I spent a lot of time reading through lists of names from a baby naming book, as I wanted a name with heartfelt meaning—not just any name.

My pregnancy was the longest nine months of my life. I was overdue by two weeks, which deep down felt like I was delaying that fateful moment.

Then, finally, the moment came and I was scared out of my brain. I felt emotionally isolated and so very alone.

The labor ward was blindingly cold and white. The pain was excruciating and shockingly sudden as the drugs for inducing labor kicked in. As a naive 16-year-old, I had no idea what a contraction was. Finally, they gave me an epidural. Even though it helped with the pain, I felt so very scared as they told me to lay still while they injected a needle into my spine.

The doctor's examination revealed that the baby was going to need coming out, and I was told they were going to cut me. I had no idea what that meant. Where and how were they going to do that? How much of me were they going to cut?

I found myself robotically agreeing. Sounds of utensils and scissors snipping followed.

But still the baby stayed stuck.

"We're going to have to use forceps," the doctor said.

He told me the first attempt didn't work, as my baby just didn't want to come out. Deep down, I didn't want this little being to come out either. This child was a part of me and losing a part of me was a lot to handle.

Mum was there holding me, not saying anything.
My poor mum! On thinking back, I guess this must have been terribly emotional for her too?

Then, the doctor maneuvered some more and finally my baby was pulled out. I didn't get to see him. He was taken from me straight away. Eventually, I had to ask Mum to find out that he's a boy.

Right at the moment that he was born, I felt the sudden permanent separation. Deep down on an emotional level, deep inside me, I could feel that he was gone.

I was wheeled out of the labor ward over to the children's ward building. I felt a surreal mixture of feelings. On one hand, I was relieved to be away from the other mums holding and feeding their babies. On the other hand, I longed to be with my baby. Instead, I was in a ward where no one seemed to have any idea of the extent or depth of what I had just been through.

I stayed in the hospital for another three emotional roller-coaster days. Tablets to stop the milk. Excessive bleeding. Daily drying of my stitches with a hair dryer. At the time, all I could think was that I didn't want to give my baby up for adoption.

When I was getting ready to be discharged, I said to my mum with my head hanging low, *"I want to see my baby just once."*

I recall the long, trepidatious walk back to the small room where they brought him to me. He was wrapped in a bunny rug and there was a card attached to the crib that read, "B-F-A" in big black letters. The letters meant "Baby For Adoption."

I had chosen names for my baby that had heartfelt meaning, depending on whether it was a boy or a girl. As he was a boy, I named him "Shane," as I could spell his dad's name and mine from the letters. It also means "Graced by God." Even though I felt that I was to be punished for my sinfulness, I wanted my baby to know he was born from great love. His name was all I had to give him as a remembrance of me.

Gutted and tears rolling down my face I silently and gently told him, *"I hope you're going to a really loving family and that you will have a great life. I want you to know that I will not ever forget you and I love you with all my heart ..."*

I was crying so hard, I felt so empty. I was holding my baby for the first and last time—a moment, an outpouring of 'infinite love.' That was—and still is—the most emotionally intense single moment of my entire life.

I returned to the small country town where I lived. People and friends had been led to believe that I'd been having a great ol' time living in the big smoke. But after a while, they sensed something was wrong with me, as I had become an insular and broken-hearted person. So I had to continue making up lies whenever people asked me how I was doing and if I was alright.

A few weeks after my return, I received an envelope from the adoption agency. My heart was in my throat as I opened it to find a handwritten letter from my baby's foster mum accompanied by eight photos. It was like winning the lotto and having my heartbroken all at the same time.

I sobbed and sobbed.

A while after that, another letter came. This time, it was to inform me that Shane had been adopted. I helplessly learned that they changed his name to "Jared."

That was 30 years ago. I have never met my son, but I am able to very specially love him at a distance.

Six years after giving birth to my son, under very different circumstances, I gave birth to my daughter. This was a planned and wanted pregnancy—I so wanted to have another child to replace the one I'd lost. I remember the profound feeling of peace that came over me when I held my daughter for the very first time. It was so unlike what I felt with my son, as I knew I would get to keep this one.

The day after my daughter was born, the midwife who'd been on duty with me came into my room and made a point of asking, *"How did you do it?"*

"Do what?" I replied, quite puzzled by her question.

The midwife wanted to know what kind of pre-natal training I'd had. When I told her I hadn't had any, she was amazed. *"In all the years I've been delivering babies,"* she said, *"I never saw anyone as calm and present and focused as you were."*

In writing this now and reflecting back, I realize that my teenage pregnancy—with all its pain and heartbreak—served me in many ways.

My pregnancy took me to Sydney, which allowed me to experience a completely new world. I gained independence and resourcefulness and became capable of physically doing things for myself.

I also developed a loving and strong relationship with my Aunty Beryl. She loved me, cared for me, gave me shelter and reassurance, loving me like a daughter. It was a different form of communication with another "mother" which, interestingly enough, has more recently helped me deepen and enrich the communication I now have with my own mum.

I am more open and truthful with my mum and can share a variety of feelings that may even bring up emotions for her. I've come to know it has the potential for her to now feel her pain and appreciate how it serves. This has helped establish that she is loved no matter what.

I realize that the extreme experience of Jared's birth enabled me to very specially appreciate the birth of my next baby and if I had given birth under normal circumstances, I would not have the rare and special friendship I have with my daughter.

The communication and appreciation I enjoy with my daughter, Rebekah, enables us to share in all kinds of ways. From our achievements and new awareness, to any challenges we may be facing. We spend quality time together, and it's equally ok for us to get on with our separate lives.

When my daughter was nine, I thought it only fair for her to know about her half-brother. I was, however, uneasy at first about revealing this information, as my mind had grown accustomed to its prison of secrecy. But when I broke my silence and shared my story with my little girl, we had a natural and easy conversation. My daughter's face lit up with delight and curiosity… and I felt ever so blessed to have her in my life.

For many years, I wondered how I could ever get over so much judgment and loss. I felt I'd done something wrong and must be punished. I judged myself very harshly with self-talk that was cruel: Good mothers don't give up their children! An unwed mother must be a slut and a disgrace to society and family!

All this started me on my journey of looking inward and practicing mindfulness. I realized that the selfless act of delivering my son to a life that was better than what I could offer required incredible courage and fortitude. The expertise I gained in navigating my subconscious has created clarity and a deep relationship with my intuition. I realize now that it is a process in motion, and there is a deeper meaning.

The agony of having and losing Jared, and all the guilt and secrecy that came with it, has led me to the heart of love. This new understanding of love has given me a sense of belonging, a profound inner calm and peace, a deep and rich appreciation of people for who they are—and, most of all, acceptance of the person I am.

My home is now on the Gold Coast in Australia, and I live with a man whom I love. My work is to help others transform their most painful experiences into sources of freedom and beauty and to live lives of empowered awareness. I feel I can now be seen without fear, without hiding or secrecy—that love has set me free.

♡♡♡

Michelle Patterson is one of Australia's leading experts in matters of the heart and facilitates educational women empowerment classes and mentoring for teens, mothers, women of all ages and business executives, to Equilibrate their most personal challenges to one of greater clarity, confidence, and purpose. From Teen Pregnancy: Trauma to Transformation http://michellepatterson.com.au

Thank God I Listened

BY MITCH RUSSO

I was cold—shivering actually—as I walked into the bathroom of John Dewey High located on Coney Island, just 2 stops from Brighton Beach on the D train. I wasn't wearing a coat this overcast February morning, just a dungaree jacket with all my patches and pins. That was my identity, how I repelled adults and challenged authority. I showed my colors. My Jimi Hendrix patch on my left arm spoke volumes while the marijuana leaf patch on my lower pocket told people I was cool.

Winter was harsh that year. I remember the ice and dirty slush covered the streets in frozen waves as busses had splashed it on sidewalks and buildings weeks ago, throughout the streets of New York. I didn't give it a second thought and, that's where I lived, in Brooklyn.

I was smoking weed pretty regularly at that point, yet still attending classes—well, most of the time. I showed up when I didn't oversleep or have something better to do. At 16, I had many better things to do, all more important than school.

This high school building was new. It was the promise of a technical high school that wasn't fulfilled. Instead, we had empty labs and vacant teachers who complained outwardly to anyone who would listen. John Dewey H.S. was an experiment in creating an environment for learning. It was nothing like what the founders had promised. It was a failure so far, but I had no control over that. I can only be responsible for what I did with it, and honestly, my plans were to get stoned and play guitar.

I entered the bathroom expecting to find a group of guys huddled around the space heater with the window open so the smoke could escape easily, in case a teacher walked in. There was a fifty percent chance the teacher would smoke with us, but we couldn't take the risk.

I figured someone would have some weed for me; someone always did. I had $5 in my pocket, and I probably should have used it for lunch, but I reasoned I could eat something later.

"Hey!" I said with a deadpan expression as I threw my backpack on the ground in an act of defiance. They knew what it meant. There was already a pile of books and backpacks strewn throughout the cold, damp bathroom space when I let my own bag drop into that pile.

"Anyone got some?" No one spoke, no one had any weed to sell, and I just wanted to get stoned. That was the common thread among the group I hung with. We wanted to get high. Race, creed, color had no bearing when you have a common interest.

One guy spoke up; Touché was the name he used. A black dude with a shiny leather coat, a beret cap and dark sunglasses that never left his face. *"I got something for you,"* he spoke. He pulled out a glassine bag, about an inch long and half an inch high. I knew what it was. I had turned him down before. He was a junkie. I knew that.

But I wanted to get high. I had skin-popped before, meaning I had injected into the back of my upper left arm, not directly into a vein, which was considered safer, but I didn't exactly know why or even if that was true.

He dumped the contents of that tiny envelope into a bent spoon, went to the sink, added a few drops of water, and then with a single movement, popped open a dented, gold-plated Zippo and cranked the flint wheel. A tiny flame struggled to catch hold under the spoon, he cooked the contents until they bubbled.

We were kids, who knew what was clean? He grabbed a syringe from his pocket and drew in the home-made stew, signaling me to roll up my sleeve. I did, he popped it into my right arm behind the muscle with a quick jab, and then a push of the plunger.

I felt the warm rush of a heroin high, which I had experienced before. This time, it was a little less powerful than the last time, as I came to realize that it always is. I gave him the $5 bill and he nodded a nod of approval as I rolled down my sleeve. I had to collect myself in stages, I was moving slowly, as I walked out of the second-floor bathroom and headed to the staircase. I knew I could sit there peacefully for a few minutes, which I did. Just as I was approaching, I felt sick; I bent over and lost whatever was left of breakfast. I knew that was, unfortunately, part of the experience.

I felt relieved in an odd way, but the deep fog that rolled over my brain was urging me to stay still a little while longer. We all knew that heroin is addictive, maybe the most addictive substance in the world. I knew this, and I also knew it could kill me, but the odds were that I would live another day.

An hour passed, and I was regaining motor movement again. I checked my schedule: I had a class I could sleep in on the third floor, and so off I went and found the half-finished, mostly empty classroom and our ambivalent teacher just getting started. I slipped my sunglasses on and slouched down in the last row.

By the time the class was coming to an end, I felt my brain coming out of the fog and back to earth. I turned in my homework, which I had completed the night before, with a nod from the teacher. I knew I would get at least a B, the work was way too easy.

Being socially inept at 16 seemed to be working for me, I played lead guitar in a band I had organized earlier last year. We practiced on Saturdays, and I knew we would be getting high after band practice. That's when the girls from the neighborhood would come by and watch. If it weren't for my band life and the guitar, I wouldn't ever have contact with girls who might want to be more than friends.

The next morning, back at school, I needed to see if I could get some weed for Saturday's band practice, and went back to the second-floor bathroom. Touché and his crew were there as always, beckoning me to join them. I asked as before: *"Got any?"* And he nodded yes, and opened his hand to another glassine bag.

I shook my head. *"No, I want some weed,"* which resulted in a short shaking of his head. He then once again pushed me to take the glassine bag. I did, and I gave him $5 as before.

I didn't use it that day. I stored it away in my wallet where I knew it would be safe until the next day, after band practice when everyone was gone. I knew that the drug had its grip on me when I found myself thinking about it all day on Saturday. As we practiced, I considered how I would enjoy the high I had waiting for me. And then, everyone left, and I was all alone.

I had my own spoon and my own Zippo lighter, and I arranged them carefully on the makeshift table consisting of two guitar amps in my mom's basement

I pulled out the sealed plastic syringe, added a few drops of water and waited for it to boil. Then, as I was about to plunge the new syringe of bubbling mixture into a vein in my right arm, something happened ...

The phone rang.

I put the syringe down, I answered the phone, I heard nothing.

"Hello? Hello? Who's there?"

Nothing.

I waited a second to see if anyone was really there. It was a dead line. I hung up.

Annoyed to have interrupted my activity, I resumed guiding the syringe on its trajectory toward my vein when I realized the syringe was frozen solid. The counterfeit, evil concoction I had cooked had cooled down and congealed into a solid block.

It was at that moment my whole life flashed in front of me: a life of despair, addiction, and poverty, an early

162   THANK GOD I WENT THROUGH HELL

demise for sure. I saw that future, and I saw that I may have been granted a reprieve.

The realization was immediate. Had that phone not have rung, I would be dead. I would have died instantly, maybe over the course of 45 to 60 seconds as the deadly poison headed straight to my heart. I sat there stunned, horrified at where my life had taken me up until this moment.

I broke down in tears. Sobbing alone in the basement of my mom's house, I had dodged a bullet. I realized then just what would have happened, and I would have forfeited a life issued to me to use as I wish.

How did that happen? What did it mean? Who called me? Was it God on the other end of that line dialing my number?

As I sobbed alone in the basement, I felt an opening of sorts—a subtle change that Saturday morning. I started to feel my feelings for the first time. I was hurt, and I was coping in the only way I knew how.

Funny how one split second of your life can change it entirely. I developed a new respect for the adults in my life. I realized how hard it was to see a kid like me, wasting his life. I became exterior to the subjective world and saw myself from a distance, and I didn't like it.

Those adults, previously enemies and antagonists, were there to help me on my journey through adolescence. I became open to that support and let them help me, not instantly but slowly as I regained trust, hard as it was.

The truth is that I never really saw my own life outside of school and home. I knew that other kids grow up into adults, but I couldn't see how that would happen for me. I started to wake up to the idea that moving on — past the drugs and into a world where I have something to offer, — could be appealing.

As I a left my teenage years, I was also able to look back and see what I gained. My experience with the drug world in the big city left me with an unexpected gift.

When I walked into that high school bathroom, I felt as if I entered Touché's "office," it was where he conducted his business. Even though he scared me on one level, there was a professionalism about what he did. I remember summoning my inner-Touché as I negotiated bookings for my band, carefully weighing my expenses vs. what my competitors were charging and the split among band members, and then holding my space in getting the deal done and delivering it.

Later, as I built my first business, I often remembered just how disciplined and structured my high school drug dealer was in his "sales" presentation and business process. Don't get me wrong, I certainly didn't admire what he did, but to succeed, everything had to work perfectly—it wasn't lost on me. I mimicked his matter-of-fact confidence and direct approach to closing as I helped Tony Robbins and Chet Holmes, as their CEO, to grow their company. I built a world-class company and touched thousands of lives.

Realizing that other kids are out there in the same position that I was, I also started speaking to groups of teenagers as part of the Hugh O'Brian Youth Leadership Organization.Thanks to where I am now, I am able to be the "gel in the syringe" for them. I would have missed all that incredible experience had I not experienced the drug world and learned my street smarts back then. I am grateful to be able to inspire others and to give back to a world that I took so much from as a boy.

♡♡♡

Mitch Russo co-founded Timeslips Corp, which grew to become the largest time tracking software company in the world before it was sold to Sage plc in 1998. Mitch went on to join long-time friend Chet Holmes as President, later to join forces with Tony Robbins and together created Business Breakthroughs, International with nearly 300 people and about $25M in sales.

In 2013, Mitch began writing "The Invisible Organization" which is the CEO's guide to transitioning a traditional brick and mortar company into a fully virtual organization.

An avid travel and landscape photographer, Mitch's work won 1st prize with The Sierra Club in 1994 and more recently was published in JETGALA Magazine with a 2-page spread. Mitch is always checking for a full moon in Iceland and has been known to disappear at a moment's notice.

Mitch's work can be seen at www.LensTraveler18.com.

Thank God I'm a Recovering -Heroin Addict

BY PAUL EFRON

"There is a crack in everything, that is how the light gets in."—Leonard Cohen

In 1980, when I was new to South Florida, I read an article in the Miami Herald about a new program in Fort Lauderdale called, Narcotics Anonymous. The article caught my attention because it featured interviews with two heroin-addicted alcoholics who had stories similar to mine. There was a phone number listed, and I dialed the number, and someone came to pick me up.

When we arrived at the meeting, I was immediately put off. It was in a makeshift church in a dingy storefront. As for the people I saw there, each looked worse than the other. Within a few minutes, I had the feeling that this was just another place where I didn't belong. I'd spent fifteen years battling my addiction– hospitalizations and suicide attempts were the normal course of business. I was two month shy of my thirty-second birthday and had long since accepted hopelessness as my life.

165

I thanked the guy who'd picked me up for bringing me, apologized for leaving so soon, and headed for the door. I wanted to get away as fast as I could.

There are those threads in a person's life which I am convinced are orchestrated by some higher order in the universe. At the exact moment I was leaving, not a minute sooner or later, someone from my past walked through the same door, except he was on his way in.

We were both pretty shocked to see one another. Marc was from the same neighborhood where I grew up in Bayside, Queens. I ended up back in the meeting, a cup of coffee in hand. Marc turned out to be the designated speaker that night, but I didn't need to listen to his story— I'd lived it with him.

We both came of age in the 1960's at the height of the Age of Aquarius. We both hung out with a "rat pack" of close buddies who were always on the cusp of trouble. Marc's arrests had been in the papers, just like mine. Marc and I started shooting heroin at the same time, and we shot up together regularly. But that evening, when Marc spoke, he told us proudly that he hadn't found it necessary to put any substances in his body for the last six months.

Six months! My ears perked up. The Marc I remembered couldn't even go six hours without putting something in his body. The only time I'd known Marc to refuse a drug was when he was already passed out.

That evening marked the start of a 180-degree turnaround in my life. After fifteen years in and out of rehab– I'd even been in a coma where my family was told, *"Don't waste your time visiting. If he happens to live, he is going to be a vegetable!"*– I finally quit for real.

And as I put to rest what had been my life, I started an unexpected new life.

One of the experiences Marc and I shared happened when the Queens DA's office orchestrated a sting on dope-dealing high school students. The cops and the newspapers made a big deal out of this. Next day, we all awoke to screaming headlines—*"Early Morning Raid Nets 23 Drug Dealers."* And on the front page of The Daily News was a picture of Marc being dragged from his mom's house. They made him, all of us, look like big-time dealers. But the worst part was that the reporter who wrote the story mentioned that Marc had had rollers in his hair. Rollers in his hair! At the time it happened, Marc was fucked—we all were! But, in retrospect, in the telling the story became hilarious.

I started speaking in front of groups and discovered an unexpected new gift—laughter! I'd been given the ability to bare my soul in front of audiences and have them laugh and cry. My greatest joy is when someone tells me how their life was transformed after hearing me speak.

All the hell I once experienced has become a tool for me to help others. I have a treasure trove of amazing stories– from when I passed out in a patch of poison ivy to when I hallucinated at a Broadway show (and thought I was part of the performance). From when I sat in a rocking chair watching a TV that didn't work (I'd just had shock treatments at Creedmoor), to my wife telling me, *"Stop trying to kill yourself by jumping off the roof ... it isn't high enough!"*

The more I was humiliated at the time, the funnier and more inspiring it is now when I share it.

What a joy it is to get standing ovations from packed audiences from Montreal to Jerusalem and all over the world! I have spent the better part of the last 35 plus years helping people get back on the right track. I have spoken in prisons and state hospitals, where I feel very much at home. And I've spoken at black-tie galas for the NYC and Palm Beach elite.

It is an overwhelmingly gratifying experience when I see someone's eyes open. The fact that I am able to write this at all is indeed a miracle.

I sit here with tears in my eyes for two reasons: One is for all the people in my life who succumbed to addiction and died from it. The other, with tears of gratitude, is for being spared and having a life today that is second to none, using a talent that would have been buried and lost … had I not been a heroin addict.

♡♡♡

Paul Efron *was born into a middle-class Jewish family in Queens, N.Y.C.- a neighborhood consumed with drugs of all kinds. He was fired from his dream Wall Street job for shooting and overdosing heroin at work.*

After fifteen years of jail, institutions and almost dying on numerous occasions, he finally found an answer through Narcotics Anonymous and became an international speaker on the disease of addiction. He has helped numerous people out of their own personal hell. He ended up becoming a partner in an N.Y.S.E. member firm,

Oncde, and became the Wall Street whiz kid of which he dreamed.

Paul has since been living the impossible dream.

Thank God For My "Eating Disorder"

BY PAULA D. ATKINSON

*I*n my 31 years on this planet, I've weighed 250 lbs., and I've weighed 80 lbs. Extremely obese as a child and teen, I almost died from starvation in college due to anorexia, bulimia, and addiction to exercise. I was the fat daughter of an alcoholic father and an extremely depressed mother.

An only child and a lonely gal, I used food to numb out. I felt like Alice in Wonderland: I didn't fit in with my family at all, and they really didn't comprehend me. Curiosity and energy filled me. The people around me seemed resentful, annoyed, and almost fearful of my desire for knowledge and insatiable hunger for stimulation. I ate to not feel. I became obese to hide and to shelter them from my obviously unacceptable characteristics.

By age sixteen I weighed 250 lbs. One day, at the start of my junior year of high school, I snapped and made the decision to be anorexic. I was definitely not a victim of anorexia. I am a person who does what she sets out to do. Years prior I concluded that my fat body directly caused every problem in my life. Now I was going to change that so I could finally be perfect. For in my head, like any overweight person, I truly believed that being fat was my only problem.

So I did it. I lost over 100 pounds in eight months by over-exercising and starving. I obtained the results I thought I wanted—I was the Homecoming Queen by my senior year, attended Homecoming with the Quarterback of the football team, and I fell deeply in love with a guy I'd had a crush on since sixth grade.

Wherever I turned, I received accolades and compliments for my "discipline" and my "hard work." No one knew that I had starved to get there. I lied to everyone all the time without a second thought. It didn't take long to realize that I couldn't stop. I would not go back to being fat, and I didn't know how to eat normally, but it would be a cold day in hell before I asked another person for help.

I continued to starve and over-exercise my way through college. I lived on hard candy, milk, and tomato juice for months. I spent so much time on the step machine at my local gym that they asked me to leave. I never set foot in the dormitory mess hall. In my dorm room, with the door locked, I chewed up and spat out hundreds of dollars' worth of food. The chewing made my mind think I was eating and soothed my rumbling tummy for a short while.

Late at night, when the dorm was quiet, I would sneak down to the garbage room to drop off grocery bags full of chewed-up food. When the gym forbade me to work out, I ran miles and miles each day on the streets. Living in San Francisco at the time, I would run up and down hills for hours and hours to burn off imaginary fat. I was completely out of control, crazy, depressed, and trapped in a hell I could have never anticipated.

The disease that I invited into my body and mind took over, and there was no room for any remnants of the person I once had been. By age twenty-one, I had starved my body down to a deadly weight. The day I arrived at the front door of a treatment center, I weighed 80 lbs. I could no longer digest solid foods—my stomach gave up, as it had been so long since I had chewed anything substantial. I stayed in the treatment center for a year while nursing my body back to a healthy weight. The re-feeding process was the most physically uncomfortable thing I have ever gone through, and I had to have more faith than I knew how to assemble.

Every day the pendulum swung between great despair and even greater trust. The most valuable lesson throughout was this new concept for me—the idea of gratitude. I had never before been grateful—not once. I had never known humility, trust, or serenity. I had never said, *"Thank you,"* and meant it—never.

That was ten years ago, and my life now isn't perfect. My food isn't perfect, my body is far from perfect, and my head still sometimes gets caught in the tornado of diet and calorie worries. My mind is like a radio stuck on an old station that I hate listening to, but I can't find the dial to turn it.

But each day I feel thankful. Each and every day, I cultivate more to be grateful for. Just as I had never known gratitude before my painful journey with my body, today I never feel a sense of victimization. The idea of "why me?" has been totally lifted. The self-obsession and the focus on what's missing from you and from me is no longer a familiar place. It's not even somewhere I visit occasionally.

Because of the painful journey I have walked in this body, I want nothing more than to be of service to those who still suffer. That is the absolute greatest gift of all. Today I am a thirty-one-year-old healthy woman with big dreams and wild hopes and a wicked sense of humor. I'm obsessed with "Hello Kitty," and have a mouth like a sailor. I think my eyes are gorgeous and my laugh is awesome. Today I appreciate who I am.

Everything good in my life is a direct result of the pain I've been through with my weight, my body, and my health. I'm a yoga teacher, a freelance writer, an author, a speaker, a successful model, and an artist. I sponsor other girls and speak in high schools and junior highs and on college campuses about addiction to diets and compulsive eating.

I am so grateful for the weight-body-food issues of my past. Today I am a healthy woman with a full and opulent life. I came to trust a while ago that gratitude is an instant and free pass to sanity and peace. After over twenty years of looking for an outside source of confidence and serenity, I now rely upon active gratitude as an immediate remedy for the bizarre idea that I'm not enough, or I don't have enough.

In my case, the feelings and habitual thoughts of lack and insecurity played out in my life through body hatred, compulsive exercise, and food addiction. One of my many dreams is to bring workshops to high schools and colleges for girls and young women. I have so much to reveal to them and such a burning wish to connect that it sometimes overwhelms me.

I want them to love themselves, as I did not. I want them to hear and take in and believe that appreciation for the body we have is the only way we can battle the culture's messages telling us that our worth depends on our body's appearance and size. When I speak from a fearlessly authentic place to young women, I see their eyes sparkle. They give themselves permission to be as wise as they naturally are. I remind them to love themselves, and that their most important job is to take care of themselves. My gratitude for them and for where I am today is contagious; they feel it and radiate it back. Together, we can all muster up the faith to be thankful for what we have. Gratitude, in my experience, is the mightiest sword against suffering and the softest way to peace.

♡♡♡

Paula D. Atkinson is a registered yoga instructor at five hundred hours, a freelance writer, and a creativity coach. Her yoga practice started in northern California, where she remembers going to yoga classes with her mother when she was very young. Then she gave it up for a decade as she grappled with obesity and anorexia, compulsive exercise, and deep depression. She has been teaching full-time for seven years in Washington, DC. She now divides her time teaching yoga, speaking at sororities and high schools about her journey, and writing freelance. Paula also facilitates creativity focus groups in her home. Paula and her partner, Carlo, live in New York City, where Paula works toward a graduate degree from Columbia University so she can reach more people with her message of hope. Please check her out at PaulaDAtkinson.com.

Thank God I Was Adopted

BY SARAH COLLINGE

*T*he atmosphere crackles with anticipation in the delivery room. Everyone present seems to share a supercharged alertness, brought about by the new life emerging from this soon-to-be mother and her very loud voice.

She screams again. This one is the worst yet.

My responsibility as a Registered Nurse overrides my impulse to focus on pity, and I check the woman's vital signs. As I witness her agony in this last push, the empathetic part of me can't help wishing she had gotten an epidural to help with the pain, if not for herself then for me.

But as an actor, I'm always observing, and there's a passionate part of me that is filing this away for later use. I find human behavior immensely fascinating, and I love to use what I learn in my craft. Today this sweat-soaked Jane Doe with anxiety etched across her face has given me some real insight. If I ever play the part of a woman in labor after seeing this, get that Oscar ready! But what happens next is something I'm just not ready for.

175

I wipe the copious scarlet from the tiny face of the newborn, and put seven pounds, four ounces of pure vulnerability into the mother's arms. Her countenance transforms as I watch all her misery turning into bliss before me. There is tightness in my chest, and I'm suddenly overcome.

In her eyes, I see all the feeling she has for her child, and I know I'm in the presence of something boundless. Something timeless. What I'm gazing into is an abyss of love.

"*Sarah.*" I hear my name as though from far away. And then more sharply. "*Sarah!*"

When I look up at the doctor, my eyes are stinging. He stares at me in surprise. He knows I'm adept at keeping my emotions in check. I slap a tear away as I flee the room, blindsided by feelings I have never dealt with.

How could my birth mother have given me away? And why?

My adoptive parents were cautious when the Agency informed them that a baby girl had just been born to a 17-year-old and was up for adoption.

"*I'm not sure I can go through it all again,*" my adoptive mother said. Six months earlier they had adopted twins, Sarah and Simon. But their birth mother had changed her mind, and they'd had to give them back after 2 weeks of thinking they were a new family. It was heartbreaking.

But as this new baby gazed up at them, they knew there was no going back.

"Can you promise us this adoption will be final?" my adoptive father had asked. The Agency promised.

Theirs had been a true love story. My father was an officer in the Royal Air Force, and Mum was a nurse. They met one Sunday in the crypt of St Clement Danes church when they were both on duty. Dad proposed a week later, and they were married within 4 months. They dearly wanted to start a family but couldn't conceive, and so they decided to adopt.

They took me home with them at 5 weeks old, chose a new name for me, and loved me as their very own. I was their daughter, and they couldn't have loved me more if I had been born of them. I was secure and happy growing up as an only child, and unaware of the significance of my adoption. Like most children, I just lived in the moment and got on with the business of growing up. My parents told me that being adopted made me special, and that sounded good enough to me!

My parents and I love each other unconditionally, yet I'm also aware they are not my flesh and blood. I have never looked into any face that resembles mine. No one is able to say how much like Aunties so-and-so I am, or predict my future talents and tendencies according to family history. Since my epiphany in the delivery room, I cannot stop the questions from coming.

Who am I? Where did I come from? Do my birth parents think about me? What is my genetic inheritance?

At 24, after much deliberation, I contact the Adoption Agency. They tell me my birth mother had hoped I would come looking for her one day, and had registered her details years ago.

"Hello," I stammer into the phone's receiver. *"This is your daughter ..."* The words are not easy to say and they echo strangely in my head. I feel a twinge of disloyalty and I correct myself, *"... your birth daughter."*

After she put me up for adoption, my biological mother had gone on to have two other children. I have a half brother and sister. She had also become a nurse! My biological father had gone on to become a doctor, and a grandfather and uncle are also doctors. Is it any wonder that I was drawn toward nursing? What strange coincidences! My mind is reeling with new information. I'm getting a sense of my genetic inheritance already, and it's a lot to digest.

Still intensely curious, I go alone to the meeting place.

"Geraldine," I hear someone call, and I take no notice. But it comes again more insistently, from behind me. *"Geraldine!"*

I turn and look into a face more similar to my own than any I have ever seen before. She takes my hand in hers, and it is so much like mine that it's almost spooky. I feel a primal attraction to her that is completely reflexive and involuntary.

"I've dreamt of this moment for so long," she says.

But even with this visceral urge to embrace my own flesh and blood at last, I feel emotionally torn. There, in her eyes, is that look of boundless maternal love I saw on that woman's face in the delivery room.

She steps forward and puts her arms around me, tears welling up.

Now I have what I thought I had come here seeking. Here is that pure, unrelenting, limitless parental adoration ... and for some unknown reason I stand here wooden, deflecting it.

I pull back, look again into my birth mother's love-struck eyes, and suddenly I'm angry.

"If you cared this much, then why?"

"One night, my mother heard me crying and came into my room. I'd been trying to conceal the pregnancy because I didn't know what to do," my birth mother tells me. *"You'd better leave home before your father finds out!"* her own mother had said. So she left her hometown and was sent to a Mother and Baby home miles away, to give birth.

"I knew I was considered too young to bring up a child on my own and back then it was taboo to be an unmarried mother. Your father was only 18, and we decided there was little choice but to put you up for adoption. It was an agony, but we thought you would have a better life."

I can't argue with this. It has proven to be true.

"Did you ever ... regret it?" I ask.

"Three weeks later, I tried to get you back," she continues, *"But they wouldn't take you away from the couple who adopted you. They said they had made a special promise. I was distraught."*

I know she had loved me and thought about me over the years, and I feel deep compassion for her as a young mum having to part with her baby. She did the best she could at the time in the most difficult of circumstances.

"Why are you still so angry?" she asks. The question catches me off guard.

"Because you look at me like only a mother can look at her child," I blurt. *"You look at me with a love that only a parent can feel."*

"Yes," she replies, *"That is how I look at you."*

"The thing that makes this hard for me," I tell her, *"is that it's familiar. It's the look my Mum gave me night and day as I tumbled through childhood. I had that. She was there, and she gave it to me."*

"But I have it for you, too ..." her words trail off. In this moment, my birth mother understands that in every sense I already have great parents, and I can't be someone else's daughter as well. I can't fulfill her dream of stepping into my life and filling a void. There is no void.

"I should not have called you Geraldine," she says. *"Your name is Sarah, and I'll just have to accept that."*

"No," I tell her, *"'Geraldine' isn't who I am, nor is 'Sarah.' I am the sum total of all my experiences and my genetic makeup. But most important of all, I am who I choose to be."*

"And who do you choose to be, dear?" my birth mother asks me.

"I'm an actress, mother," I reply, but she doesn't hear my words. She's transfixed by my facial expression. I've already used my skills to conjure up a nice parting gift for this woman who gave me life. I look at her with a love in my eyes that only a daughter can feel for her mother.

I've had a good life, and I love my parents very much. I'm blessed to have been given a stable home life where I felt safe and loved. I don't know who I might have become if I had been brought up by my 17-year-old mum, and I will never know. It was a healing process to find out more about my origins, but I couldn't change the past. I had been given unconditional love by my parents and just as I had been a gift to them, I feel they have been a gift to me.

Meeting my birth mother hasn't changed who I am. It has given me a different perspective on my life, though. It was an amazing experience, but it gradually began to dawn on me that I needn't have been asking, *'Who am I?'* just because I was adopted, because who I am now is who I choose to be.

I choose to see the universe as a perfect place wherein everything has a purpose and there are no mistakes. I choose to honor life in all its different forms and to marvel at the universal intelligence that holds it all together perfectly. I trust my instincts, my inner promptings, and feel guided in all my undertakings by something greater than myself.

I developed a passion for acting, and in every character I portray, I draw on the experiences of my soul, but with my feet firmly on the ground. All of life is a stage in a sense, and acting is a perfect medium for me to express the different aspects of myself in a purposeful and creative way. I may be asked to be Geraldine or Sarah or Ruth or Jennifer, and I can become any of them for a film, but I always feel the 'me' inside, and I know that's who I am! I also feel passionate about helping others to help themselves by sharing in any small way what I have learned along the way. I live for the moment and am grateful for all that I do have and don't dwell on all that I don't have or could have had. Who am I? I am all that I am!

It was Mother's Day, and I took Mum a big bunch of her favorite lilies.

"Thank you for adopting me, Mum, and loving me through thick and thin. I'm sorry you and Dad weren't able to have a child together, you know, your own flesh and blood. Has it ever bothered you?"

"No, darling, it never has. I can honestly say that it's never made a lot of difference to me that I didn't carry you for nine months. As far as I was concerned, you were my daughter from the moment I laid eyes on you and nothing will ever change that. We've had our ups and downs like any other mother and daughter but once a mum, always a mum, even when your kids are grown up. You'll understand that yourself now that you're a mum too."

My birth mum is, no doubt, a warm and lovely person, but she wasn't the one who was there for me every night and day as I tumbled through childhood. She isn't the one I called *"Mummy."*

$\heartsuit\heartsuit\heartsuit$

Sarah Collinge qualified as a State Registered Nurse and has worked in the UK and Australia.

She also holds diplomas in Beauty Therapy and Nutrition. No longer a practicing Nurse, she is interested in helping others to recognize and access their unique genius and to work with their own innate power to heal themselves, both physically and emotionally. She works, amongst other empowering healing modalities, with Quantum Scalar Wave laser technology, a powerful tool that facilitates healing on all levels. She has also been acting over the past 7 years and plans to one day be involved in a film dealing with adoption issues.

Sarah is Mother of two sons and lives in the south of England by the sea in Bournemouth, she is also a nanny to a young baby and works with an international adoption coach who helps couples adopt from abroad, supporting and guiding them through the process and beyond.

Thank God I Was Ugly

BY TINA MARIE JONES

I adjust my mic pack, smooth out my dress, then stroll through the drafty hallway toward the set. Two minutes left before lights ... camera ... action!

"Lucy ... you have some 'splaining' to do," one producer yells out to the tech hand nearest me. It's always hectic during the final moments before going live.

I turn to face a floor-length mirror, glancing over my attire, hair, and makeup one last time before making my entrance. Mirrors and I never used to get along. But today, I no longer see that awkward girl who stuck out like a sore thumb among her peers. A light giggle escapes my lips, and with a sly grin, I slowly eyeball my every curve, *"Girl, how did you ever think you were ugly?"*

Me, ugly? I have a light complexion, light eyes, and strawberry blonde hair.

All through childhood and adolescence, I was the "pale" one, the one who was different. The other kids were all caramel-skinned, dark-eyed, and dark-haired. Their features, I thought, were so beautifully defined. I didn't fit in.

Their stares, directed towards me, placed me in the spotlight—but adoration was not their motive. Couldn't I just be invisible?

Then there was Josie, the dominant force in our 5th-grade class who gleefully attacked anyone she saw as different with her loud mouth and derogatory comments. One time, I was traipsing through the playground when, Ooh, no ... there she was! Josie was headed straight toward me with a group of kids who were more than eager to follow and watch her in action.

I frantically searched for the nearest escape but ended up directly in her path.

She stopped abruptly, paused, and then slowly eyed me up and down. I froze. *"What's wrong with you? You don't have any eyebrows and your hair is orange! It's so ugly,"* she taunted. The laughter I heard would stay with me and become the soundtrack of my life.

Later that night, as I studied my reflection, I could see Josie standing over me spouting those heart-piercing words. My eyes welled up with tears once more. The worst part was that she was right. My frizzy, strawberry blond hair, fair skin, freckles, no eyebrows, and a pudgy body made me think of Bozo the clown. I figured I could always get a job with the circus if I ever wanted. I glared at that ugly girl and let my ghostly forehead drop to my freckled forearm. I really was a freak.

Unfortunately, junior high did not bring an improvement, but rather confirmed the miserable truth. Josie was merely a 2 on the Richter scale compared to the junior high kids. Many wanted to beat me up over my looks. Physical abuse too! It would have been better to wear long sleeves and throw a paper bag over my head.

"Don't rub up against her ... You'll get white." *"I bet they can see you from satellites, 'cause you glow in the dark, even during the day."* These were the taunts from my classmates.

Even the teachers joined in. During a history discussion on WWII, Mr. Jackson talked about the Nazis, Hitler, and the slaughtering of millions of Jews. He pointed at me and announced, *"The Aryan race looked like her."*

My cheeks burned like fire, and again, all eyes were on me. So now my appearance was also responsible for the death of Jewish people!

The wind blew the tears off my cheeks as I walked toward the town center to watch a parade with my parents. *"One cotton candy, please."* Oh, how I loved the sticky, sweet fluffiness ... a temporary escape ball of sugar. I rushed off to the restroom.

"What? No! Come on!" I tugged on that zipper for at least 5 minutes, then snap! It popped off, and I stood there with my crotch exposed, wondering how I was going to cover up. My cropped t-shirt wouldn't do the trick. What could I say? It was the 80's. My mom, I knew, would have a safety pin. I managed to maneuver through the crowds with a paper napkin covering the area. When I finally found my mom, all she could say was, *"We're going to have to stop feeding you. You're fat."*

The shame trickled through my veins like poison. I went home and told the ugly girl in the mirror, *"They want a freak ... I'll show them a freak."*

First, I used food coloring and dyed my contacts. Then, I painted streaks in my hair with markers. I wore a trash bag as a dress. I could play the role that everyone had designated for me. In fact, if I acted out the part with enough confidence and admitted to the world that I really was weird, inside and out, perhaps feeling accepted would no longer be an issue.

They accepted me all right ... the boys, that is. At the time, their compliments seemed sincere, but they were playing to my insecurities. It's amazing how quickly people learn to manipulate and prey on the most vulnerable. Maybe I just wanted to feel pretty, even once, even for a few moments. Never mind that their kindness required me to be physical. I ached for the praise and needed to hear it, even if it was a lie.

I began obsessing over the things I thought I could control. My mama's southern cooking, for example, was so delicious, but not the healthiest. Both my mom and dad were overweight, and I didn't want to end up like them, so I stopped eating. *"Oh, I'm going out with friends, so I'll eat with them,"* or *"I already ate at school,"* and *"I'm going to eat this in my room."* I invented any excuse possible to avoid consuming calories. I knew I had to eat something, so water, black coffee, celery, and carrots became my daily nourishment. I was only fifteen and downing 1012 Dexatrim per day. This continued for over a year.

Makeup and pills became true and constant companions. They serviced me beautifully. My eyebrows finally stood out, and my freckles remained hidden. There weren't many options for mousse back then, so I had to buy Afro Sheen, but who cares? It tamed the wild beast on top of my head. I even had a boyfriend, Forrest, who seemed to appreciate me for my true self.

High school marked a turning point for me; no more misery, as long as I stuck to the plan. *"Tina,"* snap, snap. *"Are you all right?"* The blurriness slowly dissipated, and the hard, cold tiles underneath my fragile body startled me a bit. A small group of classmates encircled me, but Forrest was right by my side, smiling at me with one hand holding mine, while the other hand held my head. I fainted 23 times per week on average. Switching to Slimfast apparently didn't balance my blood sugar levels, but I could handle the fainting. I could even handle the excruciatingly painful migraines. But when my period disappeared, the real worry set in.

Forrest and I were sexually active and certainly not ready to play house. My parents set up appointment after appointment with every doctor imaginable.

They provided my folks with no answers or solutions because I refused to share any of my secrets. I had made a deal with that ugly girl in the mirror a long time before, and I was not about to dishonor our agreement. I exercised to that damn Jane Fonda video like crazy. The sweat poured out of me as I reached for the ceiling with both arms stiff and straight, then I pulled them back down to my side as I lifted each knee to my chest. *"81, 82, 83, 84! ..."* No giving up now.

"You're going to exercise yourself to death!" my mom exclaimed. If only that were enough. The only opinion I really wanted was Forrest's.

I could actually spend time alone with him without wearing much makeup, or smoothing out my hair and covering up my white skin. We walked to the park one day, hand in hand, snapping pictures of nature, people, and anything else that interested us. I was not particularly dolled up, but it didn't really matter. We approached a wooden bench where I plopped myself down and stared up at the sky, silently asking it about my future. Forrest pointed the camera at me, and I begged him not to take a picture, but he did anyway.

"This is totally you." I was afraid to look, and at first glance, I cringed, but then looked again and saw the playful personality that he had captured. I was silly and completely unaware of who I really was, but he valued me the same. *"Hey Tina, I want you to stop what you're doing ... You're killing yourself."*

The next day in class, I just sat there very still, completely zoned out, repeating his words over and over in my head. *"Tina?"* My heart skipped a beat as I realized that Ms. Sain was calling me up to her desk. I wasn't in trouble, right? No ... a straight 'A' student like me ... no way. I hesitantly walked over to her and tried to slow down my breathing and keep my knees from knocking.

"You know who you remind me of?" she asked. I shrugged my shoulders and gave her a half smile. *"Lucille Ball,"* she told me, and I said, *"Thanks"* and then awkwardly returned to my seat.

Lucille Ball? Was it the orange hair we had in common? Lucille Ball? *I Love Lucy* ... Ricky Ricardo ... Fred and Ethel. All sorts of images flashed through my mind as I recalled the many reruns I'd watched over the years. She really was a phenomenal comedian, entrepreneur, and entertainer. Did Ms. Sain really notice any of Lucille's traits in me? I struggled to accept her sincere compliment.

If that's what she meant then perhaps, just maybe, I was destined to be somebody. When I crawled into bed that night, I retraced the picture Forrest took of me and began to recognize something else. I definitely possessed a look unlike any other. But could I actually see beauty in my vulnerability?

I met with one more doctor, and this time, something clicked. After asking some questions and doing a quick examination, he gave us his suggestions. I sincerely hoped that he wouldn't announce to my parents that I had an eating disorder. He never uttered those words, but I can only presume he knew the truth for he suggested a nutrition plan. It ended up being a gift. There were so many meal options to choose from that I felt like I hadn't lost any control, but gained a healthy perspective on food. I actually bought a wok and started cooking for my family.

Once I realized that I could achieve my goals in a healthy way, the need to sabotage myself eventually dissolved. I was proud to have turned my life around and have a positive effect on both my parents' lifestyles.

Unfortunately, both of them had left this world by the time that I was twenty five. But as much as I grieved for them, their passing forced me to grow up. My mom and dad had been my driving force. When they died, I realized I could feel good about myself and not do things just to seek approval.

The universe created a perfect balance so that even though I was losing, I was also gaining.

To this day, I still color in my eyebrows, but who cares? That's why makeup was created. The point is that I've accepted my strengths and weaknesses and can see the perfection in all of it. It took a few minutes to reach this level of thinking, but the switch finally turned on, once certain teachers and high school sweethearts put me in my place. I'm not surprised I became a comedian, a woman who loves photo shoots, an entrepreneur, an author, a TV personality, and a mother as well.

They used to stare at me as a kid ... they might as well keep on starin'. Now, when I look in the mirror, I see a woman on a mission who can go out in public without any makeup—and a beautiful woman at that. Thank you, Lucy, for paving the way for us "Gingers" and bringing me back to life.

The applause begins, the spotlight focuses in, and the announcer roars,

"AND NOW ... TINA MARIE JONES!"

♡♡♡

Tina Marie Jones-St.Cyr is a globally recognized corporate trainer, speaker and transformational coach who engages her audiences with thought-provoking questions and takes each person on a personal journey inside their unique human experience.

Her talks have been featured on stages throughout the world, in board rooms, and in family living rooms. Her interactive style, along with peppered humor, create a lively and connecting atmosphere for change and growth. A best-selling author, celebrated radio and tv personality, and an award-winning transformational growth speaker, Tina

Marie welcomes the opportunity to connect with your organization, community, and family.

www.tinamarie.com

HAVE YOU ALSO BEEN THROUGH HELL AND BACK AND HAVE A STORY OF GRATITUDE TO SHARE?

*H*ave you overcome being overweight, raped, abused, dying, dealing with the death of a loved one, being cheated on or any other devastating challenge? Your story can help other people heal their lives.

Would you love to be featured in an Amazon #1 Best Selling book series alongside N.Y. Times Bestselling Authors?

If your story is accepted into our series, our Hollywood and Broadway-trained scriptwriters expertly coach you to write your story brilliantly.

Please submit your story and apply for an interview through clicking on one of the relevant links to your personal story:

Thank God I Went Through Hell: I Was Fat
https://equilibration.net/tgi-was-fat-story-submission

Thank God I Went Through Hell: I Was Depressed
https://equilibration.net/tgi-was-depressed-story-submission

Thank God I Went Through Hell: I Was Raped
https://equilibration.net/copy-of-thank-god-i-was-raped-story-submisssion

Thank God I Went Through Hell: I Was Abused
https://equilibration.net/tgi-was-abused-story-submisssion

Thank God I Went Through Hell: I Died
https://equilibration.net/thank-god-i-went-through-hell-i-died

Thank God I Went Through Hell: I Grieved a Loved One
https://equilibration.net/thank-god-i-grieved-story-submission

Thank God I Went Through Hell: My Child Died
https://equilibration.net/thank-god-my-child-died-story-submission

Thank God I Went Through Hell: I Was Cheated On
https://equilibration.net/thank-god-i-was-cheated-on-story-submission

Thank God I Went Through Hell: General Story Submission
https://equilibration.net/thankgodi-story-submission

We look forward to speaking to you about your story.
Contact Us : info@thankgodi.com
www.thankgodi.com

www.ingramcontent.com/pod-product-compliance
Lightning Source LLC
LaVergne TN
LVHW051629080426
835511LV00016B/2261